Mission, Vision, and Values in
American Community Colleges:

# NOBLE
# AMBITIONS

By Daniel Seymour

# Mission, Vision, and Values in American Community Colleges:

# NOBLE AMBITIONS

By Daniel Seymour

Community College Press®
A division of the American Association of Community Colleges
Washington, DC

Seymour, D. (2013). *Mission, vision, and values in American community colleges: Noble ambitions*. Washington, DC: Community College Press.

Designer:  Brian Gallagher Design
Printer:  Global Printing

Community College Press® is a division of the American Association of Community Colleges (AACC), the primary advocacy organization for the nation's community colleges. The association represents close to 1,200 two-year, associate degree–granting institutions and more than 13 million students. AACC promotes community colleges through five strategic action areas: recognition and advocacy for community colleges; student access, learning, and success; community college leadership development; economic and workforce development; and global and intercultural education. Information about AACC and community colleges may be found at www.aacc.nche.edu.

ISBN 978-0-87117-398-0

*Printed in the United States of America.*
*First Edition, First Printing*

MIX
Paper from
responsible sources
FSC
www.fsc.org
FSC® C068100

# CONTENTS

# FOREWORD

For the past quarter century, I have been one of those policy wonks trying to figure out how to judge whether a college is doing a good job. People who work at colleges, especially the faculty, tend to be annoyed by those of us who ask about effectiveness, because it seems like it should be obvious. They have earned their bona fides in their disciplines. They have succeeded in attracting students. What more do I need to know?

Nowhere are the instructors more annoyed by the question than at community colleges, which tend to enroll the neediest of populations with the fewest resources. And I understand why: It seems almost insulting to ask them for an explanation of purpose, like asking a nun at an orphanage for a mission statement. But it is precisely because the needs are so great, and the resources limited, that community colleges in particular need to know —and be able to explain— what guides their decisions about who to serve and how.

"Open access" is not an adequate explanation, since institutions serve only the students who happen to discover and are attracted to the courses, programs, locations, and schedule a college happens to offer. Likewise, "student demand" does not explain what is offered, because there is no way for prospective students (imagine young adults hanging out on a street corner) to express demand for programs that don't exist but could theoretically be offered.

A community college can choose to subsidize more or fewer career–technical programs as opposed to transfer courses; it can offer English or electrician training, chemistry or calligraphy, archery or astronomy. It has a choice. *Why* does the community college do what it does? Why does it continue to do this year what it did last year? What evidence does it consider in making its decisions?

Daniel Seymour makes the case for taking seriously the task of developing meaningful, ambitious, and actionable mission, vision, and values statements at community colleges. What informs the decisions trustees make? What public purposes guide the president, faculty, and staff in their daily activities? How would the trustees and the public know that the institution's resources are strategically arrayed to achieve the goals? Colleges and faculty can too easily be accused of being knee-jerk protectors of the status quo. A robust, shared, operating vision for the college helps to make clear how the public interest, not personal interests, determine the steps that the college takes.

In making the case for planning that is truly strategic and potentially transformative, Seymour shows, with examples, the power of developing an institutional vision, a description of the college doing its job better in the future. "While the mission validates, the vision energizes." Most community college web sites explain what the college does, sometimes how. To motivate the college's constituencies, leaders also need to explain why. Doing so will make the college more effective, more likely to achieve the vision. Conveniently, it will also make it easier to answer those annoying questions from outsiders.

Robert Shireman

*Robert Shireman is currently the Executive Director of California Competes, a nonprofit project aimed at addressing the state's higher education challenges. Previously, he served as deputy undersecretary of education in the Obama Administration, where he spearheaded the successful effort to reform student lending and simplify the financial aid process, leading to his being awarded a 2012 Money Magazine "hero" award for his work on college affordability.*

# INTRODUCTION

More than 10 years ago, I was doing consulting work for a college that I will refer to as Main Street Community College. A new strategic plan needed to be developed, and the college was also about to begin preparing for regional reaccreditation. In addition, a new president had been appointed earlier in the year following the extended tenure of a well-respected predecessor. A facilities bond had been passed, too, that would allow for some much-needed capital improvements with an emphasis on integrating new technologies into the buildings. In short, there was a real sense of seriousness around the development and implementation of a strategic plan that would provide direction for the college and its stakeholders.

The workshop that I was asked to facilitate was the kick-off event. My charge was twofold: First, I was to provide a review of strategic planning concepts and language and, second, I was to motivate and inspire the several dozen individuals in attendance. Many people in higher education acknowledge the need to have a strategic plan, even if that means simply to say to accreditors and others that we have one. But most institutions also don't live and breathe the plan. So, a review of the basic components of strategic planning and a description of some best practices were appropriate. Invigorating the crowd—all of whom had come to the workshop with a long list of things they would rather be doing—was a bit more of a challenge. Understanding the need to do something does not necessarily make the task more joyful. Early in the day, therefore, I decided to introduce a series of concepts that, while not joy-inducing, at least had specific institutional and perhaps personal meaning—mission, vision, and values. The first slide provided a general definition of mission: "A mission statement should guide the actions of the organization, spell out its overall goal, provide a sense of direction, and guide decision making."

I asked people a few questions, such as "Is the mission of an institution an important concept?" and "Can it really provide guidance and help decision makers?" The general sense was that missions were very important and, indeed, perhaps even more important to institutions such as community colleges that might be seen as more mission-driven. We quickly reached consensus—mission statements were a good thing. I then asked people to talk about their college's current mission. Now, keep in mind, this was not the hard work and heavy lifting associated with developing a completely new mission statement or even tinkering with the old one. Since missions are board-approved and an integral part of all regional accreditation criteria, my straightforward, if naïve, request was merely to ask them to discuss their college's existing mission statement.

The conversation started slowly. There were a few broad observations that contained references to workforce education or general education and transfer coupled with the seemingly requisite references to "quality" and "excellence." I pressed on. I said, "A mission statement really answers the simple question, 'Why do we exist?'" The conversation stumbled forward. But it soon became obvious that no one in the room really had a clear grasp of the basic elements of their institution's mission. The conversation ended.

The next slide defined vision: "A vision statement is an aspirational description of what an organization would like to achieve or accomplish in the long term." Not surprisingly, everyone was enthusiastic about the concept. The question, "What do we want to create?" should evoke inspired and imaginative views of what is possible. But when it came time to discuss the institution's current statement of what that future should be, the room became awkwardly quiet and subdued. Some people squinted and looked skyward for divine intervention; a few tried to covertly access the college's website in order to discover the truth.

The final exercise involved values. To begin, I again gave them a simple definition for their consideration: "Important and enduring beliefs or ideals shared by members of a culture about what is good or desirable and what is not. Values exert major influence on the behavior of an individual and serve as broad guidelines in all situations." Values were again seen as being important. Perhaps the idea that they self-select into working in organizations that have a purpose other than "increasing shareholder value" was part of the equation, but individuals were sincere about the significance of building a culture in which a set of values, or enduring beliefs, were present. Unfortunately, the follow-up question, "What do you believe at Main Street Community College?" produced an unsatisfactory result. Given than many institutions, including Main Street, often enumerate a list of words such as *trust* or *diversity* in their stated beliefs, I suppose it was not surprising that the resulting discussion was more like an adult game of hide and seek: "I think 'collaboration' is in there. No, wait, it's 'teamwork.'" "Integrity' is on the list. I am pretty certain. If it isn't, it should be." "We need more 'accountability.' That's there. Isn't it?"

I am not alone in my observations. Not too long ago, Robert Sevier, a senior vice president for strategy with the consulting firm Stamats related a story at an annual conference of a national higher education association (see Carlson, 2010). He was in a meeting at which the management team at one college was "ranting and raving" about the excellence of its vision statement, keeping in mind that a vision statement should differentiate a college from its closest competitors. "So I read their vision to them, and I said, 'What do you think?' And they said, 'It's great; it's wonderful.'" Then he told them he hadn't read their vision statement—he'd read their competitor's.

Why are these stories important? What do they suggest about the relative importance that three simple questions could have in advancing the hopes and efficacy of America's community colleges? Why do we exist?, What do we want to create?, What do we believe?

Noted academicians such as Karl Weick (1976) and Henry Mintzberg (1983), among others, have described colleges and universities as being perfectly designed to resist transient forces in their environment. These "loosely-coupled" systems and "professional bureaucracies" are filled with highly certificated individuals who operate almost as independent entrepreneurs in their respective departments and classrooms. The resulting pigeon-holing process means that these institutions are largely immune to most disturbances or changes that cause other organizations to often operate in a reactive mode. As such, this resilience can be a positive attribute in many circumstances. The problem arises when the landscape begins to shift more suddenly. Resilience, under these conditions, is often perceived as intransigence. Whether the headlines involve relentless tuition increases, the skills gap versus jobs gap, being "academically adrift" due to limited learning, stunningly low completion rates, or questioning whether a college education itself is a worthy investment, that landscape is fracturing under our feet. The positive aspects of a loosely coupled structure become more of a hindrance when the institutions need to develop and pursue a more integrated response to the dynamic conditions they face.

Perhaps the best, intuitive description of what should happen next is found in the work of Robert Fritz (1989, 1999) and Peter Senge et al. (Senge, Roberts, Ross, Smith, & Kleiner, 1994). The tendency for all systems is to seek equilibrium. Usually, that means embracing the status quo or tinkering at the edges. Why? Because, as we all know, the business of challenging assumptions is incredibly difficult and often unrewarding work. Moreover, the act of "unfreezing" is especially challenging when the forces for change are perceived as being initiated by outside influences. Fritz described the resulting path of least resistance by starting with a simple story. When people came to his native Boston, they often asked him, "How did they design the layout of the roads?" If you have ever been to Boston you know that there appears to be no recognizable city planning. Of course the answer is that the roads are merely cow paths that were paved over. The hills were there first. The structure of the land gave rise to the cows' pattern of behavior in moving from place to place, and paths were formed. And then the people paved the cow paths. As Fritz noted, once a structure exists, energy moves through that structure by the path of least resistance:

> This is true not only for cows, but for all of nature. The water in a river flows along the path of least of resistance. The wind blowing through the concrete canyons of Manhattan takes the path of least of resistance. Electrical

currents, whether in simple devices, such as light bulbs, or in the complex circuitry found in today's sophisticated computers along paths of least resistance. (1989, p. 4)

For organizations to alter their course, then, the key is to develop a core competence that enables them to confront this natural tendency to seek equilibrium. This can be done by developing a desired state that differs fundamentally from the actual state. The resulting discrepancy produces a structural tension that is the opposite of equilibrium—or a state of nonequilibrium. Structural advancement can then be achieved as we choose to resolve the tension by moving along a new pathway to a desired state. In essence, the pull of a bright tomorrow is more appealing than the tug of a dull today. Figure I.1 shows these competing relationships.

For today's largest sector of higher education in this country, the

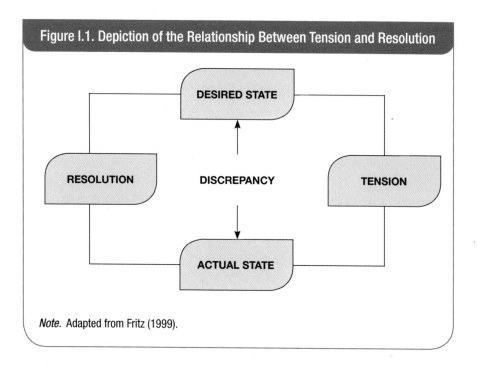

Figure I.1. Depiction of the Relationship Between Tension and Resolution

*Note.* Adapted from Fritz (1999).

current or actual state has become increasingly problematic. Whether the issue is the constant drumbeat of doing more with less or the stridency of the completion agenda discussions, the option of inaction or detached quietude seems less and less tenable. But, again, who or what can provide the structural tension necessary by describing a desired state that can generate real change?

I believe that the answer to the "who" part of that question must be "us". While the seeds of change are usually external, any lasting adaptations within an organization are those that are cultivated by and ultimately embraced by the culture itself. Modifications or alterations to the status quo that are perceived as being done to us, rather than by us, ultimately face the full wrath of organizational members who are practiced in the useful art of digging in their heels. And the "what"? I believe the answer may lie in our colleges' missions, vision and values. "Mission" comes from the Latin word *missio* meaning "sent off, to send." It reflects a fundamental reason for existence. *Vision* comes from the Latin *videre* or "to see" and seeks to describe an authentic image. Finally, values means to "to be worth" and comes from the French verb *valoir*. It is associated with worthiness. Together, they reflect an earnest desire for some type of achievement or distinction—our purposes, our aspirations, our beliefs—and the willingness to strive for their attainment. Together, they produce a desire for exertion or activity. Together, they describe a gestalt that is a desired state—our noble ambition.

With such a destination in mind, there is every reason to believe that institutions can then move along a path of least resistance in a more coordinated and strategic fashion. There is a better place. There is a better way, and it is worth fighting for. Without that pull, however, the forces of inertia take hold with a vise-like grip. It becomes easy to simply continue doing what has been done. Our institutional cow paths of yesterday become the streets we trudge along today and tomorrow in our everyday work lives.

*Noble Ambitions* is a critical examination of these issues. It is grounded in a qualitative study of more than 200 community colleges. As the title suggests, this book is ambitious. It, too, represents an earnest desire to describe in rich detail how mission, vision, and values can be used to propel institutions forward in contrast to my less-than-ambitious workshop at Main Street Community College.

- Chapter 1 describes the methodology used to generate the data and then how the resulting information was analyzed and interpreted. Further, the initial analyses of the information yield a set of observations that apply generally to how community colleges articulate their ambitions.
- Chapters 2, 3, and 4 focus specifically on the tension-creating elements of that ambition: mission, vision, and values. The core of each chapter is devoted to descriptive analyses of the textual data generated from the sample. Each chapter's conclusion pulls together various highlights and themes for the reader.
- Chapter 5 explores the idea that the real value of these elements— besides describing a desired state—is in aligning these elements with the strategic intent of the institution. After all, creating structural tension is only half the battle; the other half is in describing a new path of least resistance that enables the institution to take action and resolve the nonequilibrium in a direction toward our desired state. The three chapters associated with a mission, vision, and values become the desired state that creates the discrepancy with the actual state. That noble ambition, in turn, creates the necessary tension and nonequilibrium that is shown in Figure I.1. Resolution of this tension in provided on the (left side) in the form of a community college's strategic planning efforts that enumerate a series of action items. When noble ambition and strategic intent are tightly linked, they are a pathway that energizes and excites stakeholders. The twin concepts of tension and resolution work together as a ratchet that challenges the status quo while providing a compelling future that can engage the entire institution.
- Chapter 6 is a sharp departure from the previous ones. Stepping back from the descriptive examination of textual data across 226 community colleges, an effort is made to derive a set of nine prescriptive practices that can be considered by institutions in their desire to pursue a noble ambition. The practices are both reflective and actionable. They require the reader to challenge her or his own assumptions about how things are and what is needed to create a more compelling future. These are cow-path-busting ideas.

Finally, the Merriam-Webster dictionary defines useful as "capable of being put to use; *especially*: serviceable for an end or purpose <*useful* tools>." My chief motivation in conducting this research and interpreting the results has been focused on one simple goal: To produce something that can be put to use. Each and every community college in this country can have a noble ambition. But having a noble ambition and delivering on that prophecy are two very different things: Talking is not doing. I hope this book and its many detailed observations and promising practices will accomplish what Abraham Lincoln had in mind when he said, "The best way to predict the future is to create it." The future that American community colleges want and need is there for the making.

# CHAPTER 1

# METHODOLOGY AND OVERVIEW OF FINDINGS

## Sampling Procedure and Research Design

The scale of the community college enterprise in American higher education is huge. The fact that these institutions are relatively affordable, provide open access, and that more than 40% of the students are of the first generation to attend college also speaks loudly to how they see their role in advancing learning, quality of life, and economic development. Conducting a census of these institutions was prohibitive given the sheer number of colleges involved in granting associate degrees. Since sampling was necessary, then, I next decided to begin with a stratification exercise. Stratification is the process of dividing members of the population into homogeneous subgroups before sampling. This exercise can improve the representativeness of the sample by reducing sampling error. Table 1.1 shows the selection criteria I used.

| Table 1.1: Selection Criteria for Sampling U.S. Public 2-Year Colleges | | | |
|---|---|---|---|
| | Size | | |
| **Location** | **large** | **medium** | **small** | **Total** |
| City | 124 | 95 | 99 | 318 |
| Suburban | 73 | 51 | 57 | 181 |
| Town | 4 | 33 | 172 | 209 |
| Rural | 25 | 75 | 267 | 367 |
| Total | 226 | 254 | 595 | 1,075 |

Note. From NCES (2011).

A quick look at this table illustrates the potential challenge. Of 1,075 institutions, more than half (595) have fewer than 5,000 students (small), and 439 of these are located in town or rural settings. In contrast, there are 226 institutions that have more than 10,000 students (large), and 172 are located are in city and suburban areas. Of these, 65 colleges serve more than 20,000 students. If there is any reason to believe that the size and setting of an institution might impact its mission, vision, and values, then weighting the sample might help to improve both the analyses and conclusions. As can be seen in Table 1.2, I examined 226 institutions out of 1,075 (21%).

| Table 1.2: Stratification Criteria for Sampling U.S. Public 2-Year Colleges | | | | |
|---|---|---|---|---|
| | Size | | | |
| Location | large | medium | small | Total |
| City | 27 | 15 | 19 | 61 (19%) |
| Suburban | 21 | 11 | 11 | 43 (24%) |
| Town | 4 | 5 | 32 | 41 (20%) |
| Rural | 6 | 18 | 47 | 71 (19%) |
| Total | 58 (25%) | 59 (23%) | 109 (18%) | 226 (21%) |

Next, I used a convenience sampling approach to generate the specific colleges within each cell. Not included are institutions, mostly in Florida, that have been allowed to award bachelor's degrees. Their exclusion is based upon the need to conduct a fair comparison of institutional types. Also excluded are multicampus districts, because the real value of this analysis is in the data for the individual 2-year public college—all 1,075 of them. I did not include the smaller number of private 2-year institutions because of the for-profit nature of their missions.

I then searched the websites of these institutions. There were several reasons to conduct the research in this manner. Conducting a survey (by telephone, mail, or e-mail) of institutions of any kind would have been extremely complicated and time consuming starting with a simple, vexing question: "Who would be the institutional contact?" Just as importantly, an institution's website now fills many roles: it is a marketing tool; it responds to legal and accreditation mandates; it is a repository of the past actions; and it is an incredibly efficient process tool—how to register, how to order a transcript, how to appeal a grade and so on. Many of the larger institutions receive as many as one million hits on their website each month. In addition to searching for references to mission, vision, and values, I attempted to determine whether the statements were standalone or were connected to broader strategic planning efforts. The key reason for extending the analysis to include this was to explore whether or how the foundational questions of a noble ambition (discussed in chapters 2, 3, and 4) were connected in any meaningful way to a bias for action or strategic intent (discussed in chapter 5).

I conducted these comparisons and analyses by using content analysis software (Concordance). While the latest software used by linguists to analyze text includes many sophisticated functions, I focused on word frequency analysis and the ability to generate context. An obvious example of the use of word frequency would be in analyzing mission statements. For example, if *access* and *open access* are key terms for community colleges, to what degree are those terms explicitly used in a college's mission statement? In contrast, a more recently developed goal or institutional outcome might be *global citizenship*. Again, to what degree is that term being used? Concordances are sometimes described as KWIC (key word in context). The word *sustainable* might be used in the context of academic program design, for example, or it might be used to describe waste management practices. My analysis enumerates each time the term *sustainable* is used in the text and provides four or five words both before and after the key word in order to be able to understand the context within which it was used.

Earlier I stated that I employed a convenience sample to reach the required number of institutions within each cell. I should note that early in the process I discovered that the websites of a significant number (24%) of colleges yielded little or no information at all. No mission statement. No stated vision. No enumeration of values. I obtained that result even after using the index and search functions on each website. Since the primary focus of the examination was to provide actionable research, it was more important to look at institutions that did indeed have information to analyze. Therefore, the minimum requirement to be included in the data set was a stated mission on the college's website.

## Overview of How Colleges Present Themselves on Their Websites

My initial observations fall into three categories: the presence or absence of mission, visions, values and information; their location; and, finally, the use of proxies or other representations. While all institutions in the data set had a mission statement, only 65% also had both other elements. This result was not evenly distributed across all institutions. Larger institutions tended to have fuller descriptions of their ambition while smaller institutions tended to be leaner. That is not to say that the information was totally nonexistent but, rather, there would be only one or two elements, as an example, and they would be buried in the course catalog or in the board minutes.

Mission, vision, and values are the essence of the institution. They represent purpose, hope, and beliefs. If they aren't presented in any meaningful way on a college's electronic home, it is hard to imagine that they play any real role in the day-to-day operations of the institution. Documenting and displaying the information, as I illustrated in the Introduction, is the easy part.

One explanation for this finding is the concept of organizational slack. Community colleges are not generally known for their abundance of human and capital resources. They run pretty lean. But larger institutions may at least have the ability to create some positions that are somewhat shielded from the day-to-day operations of admitting students, advising students, teaching students. The resulting "wiggle room" or slack can afford some individuals or small groups the luxury of thinking longer term or seeing the larger picture. Reflecting on the core issues of mission, vision, and values takes an investment of time and energy. It requires thoughtful exchanges and deep dialogue among stakeholders who are vested in the enterprise. Larger institutions or ones that are more organized around ongoing reflective practices may have individuals charged with the responsibility to initiate these discussions and keep them viable and visible.

In contrast, individuals at smaller institutions undoubtedly feel overwhelmed on a regular basis with job descriptions written more broadly with an abundance of multiple responsibilities and references to "other duties as required." There is little time for reflection in such environments. Immediacy trumps thoughtful consideration. It is very difficult, even if you know a task is of longer-term importance, to devote time to a values clarification exercise, for example, when the financial aid lines are wrapped around the building and the phone lines are blinking like a distress beacon.

A logical follow-up question is this: If references to mission, vision, and values were found on colleges' websites, where were they located? It was rare, indeed, to find any direct reference to these elements on the institution's homepage. The standard click-through path or breadcrumb was to begin with an area on the vertical or horizontal navigation labeled About Us or General Information. The only exceptions to this general finding were the occasional pathways that began under Prospective Students, President, or Board Policies. Following the About Us breadcrumb usually revealed a moderately long list—alphabetized—of items such as Accreditation, Fast Facts, and Board of Trustees. Within this list could often be found one of the following references: mission, mission statement, mission and history, mission and vision, and mission, vision, and values.

If the core elements of the institution's ambition—its mission, values and vision—should be prominent in its most important communications vehicle, then a direct and easy pathway from About Us to Mission, Value, and Vision would seem to be desirable. It sends a message that we, as an institution, take these concepts seriously and we want everyone to know and understand what we are all about, where we hope to go, and the ideals we hold most dear. The problem arises when this message gets buried deep in a layer cake of data. For example, a pathway that goes General Information > About Us > Accreditation > Mission > Mission, Vision, and Values is telling the reader how we prioritize things.

The same problem of priorities manifested itself in a different way. Usually, when references to mission, vision, and values were found under About Us, the list was mercifully short and displayed in alphabetic order. But far too often the college's ambition was a bit player in a seemingly endless barrage of information, as was illustrated in one college's website (see Figure 1.1). Notice that within the unalphabetized 28-element menu, Mission, Vision, Values is buried in a list that includes restaurant and hotel recommendations. This communicates priorities to stakeholders that are probably not what the institution intended.

While there were minimal references to the elements of a noble ambition on homepages, there was the fairly consistent use of a tagline to suggest an overall sense of purpose. As Table 1.3 shows, most of these taglines appeared to fall into two simple categories: one that connoted direction and the other what I call a "word trifecta." While there is certainly nothing wrong with a little zip or marketing panache on a college's website, the concern should be that a slogan might be employed as a substitute for the hard work associated with asking and answering foundational questions about the institution's ambition or desired state.

### Figure 1.1: Sample Dropdown Menu on a College's "About Us" Tab

| About Us | About Us (cont'd) |
|---|---|
| Academics | Accreditation |
| Programs of Study | Regional Centers |
| Admission | Purchasing & Bids |
| Register for Classes | Maps & Directions |
| Tuition & Aid | Facilities |
| Student Life | Human Resources |
| Athletics | Police Department |
| News & Events | Information Technology |
| At a Glance | McAninch Arts Center |
| Mission, Vision, Values | Waterleaf Restaurant |
| Office of the President | The Inn at Water's Edge |
| Board of Trustees | WDCB Radio |
| Financial Documents | Outstanding Faculty Members |
| Administration | Tobacco Free |

| Table 1.3: Sample Taglines on Community College Websites | |
|---|---|
| **Directions** | **Trifectas** |
| A Great Place to Start | Imagine. Believe. Achieve. |
| Education for a Lifetime | Learning. Serving. Enriching |
| Achieving Dreams. | Dream. Learn. Do. |
| Your Future is our Mission | Embracing. Educating. Empowering. |
| Futures Made. Here. | Discover. Connect. Advance. |
| Climb Higher. | Define. Believe. Achieve. |
| Start Here. . . Go Anywhere! | Dream. Learn. Achieve. |

# Conclusion

Much has been written about the mission of community colleges as they have evolved over the last century. But once the unit of analysis changes from community colleges in general to individual colleges, the challenge begins. Furthermore, once mission is expanded to include other elements of a college's ambition, the essence of the challenge should be apparent. This is really about the everyday lives of hundreds of thousands of faculty, staff, and administrators and their students, not about sweeping statements made for public consumption.

Upon further examination, institution-specific ambitions should follow a three-stage process: developing, communicating, and living. Institutions must begin by making the investment in crafting their mission, vision, and values statements. We must assume that nearly all institutions have them. But my results show that communicating those results to an institution's stakeholders—internal and external—are not often being accomplished in any meaningful way. The final stage in this process provides a cautionary note. All of these data and discussions are focused on statements—the written words. But a mission statement is not a mission, a vision statement is not a vision, and a values statement is not values. The former are documented on a website while the latter can only be lived.

# CHAPTER 2

## COMMUNITY COLLEGE MISSION STATEMENTS

### Principles Underlying Mission

The study of organizations has many different approaches. One fundamental approach is to distinguish between those that are for-profit companies versus nonprofit organizations. Within this context the concept of mission has an interesting trajectory. Most of the expansive research and writing on companies that populate both the academic and popular press has traditionally paid relatively little attention to the discussion of mission or purpose. While the idea of articulating the company's purpose of existence would seem to be of primary importance, it is not reflected in the literature. A quick search of the *Harvard Business Review* database illustrates the point. For every reference to the word *mission* there are 20 references to another, more muscular term, *strategy*. This powerful trend started in earnest with Michael Porter's *Competitive Strategy* (1980), which begins with the all-encompassing statement, "Every firm competing in an industry has a competitive strategy, whether, explicit or implicit."

What is key to this straightforward opening sentence, and what has driven so much of the business world's attention over the intervening three decades, is that *strategy* is seen as a set of activities that enable a company to develop a competitive advantage that, in turn, drives important corporate metrics such as market share and profit. Strategy— what we do and how we do it—allows the firm to position itself uniquely from its rivals by deciding what different activities it needs to perform, or how to perform similar activities in different ways. Strategy, then, is about deciding. It is about consciously choosing ways to be unique and then executing on that distinctiveness in a competitive environment over a longer period of time. It is about being active, engaged, and sharp-eyed—being strategic.

This focus on strategy has taken many different forms as well. In many companies now there is a chief strategy officer. It also means that planning is now strategic planning, which encompasses environmental scanning, competitive analysis, and other methods to help individual firms understand their ecosystems. Strategy, since it is about decision-making, has also come to rely more and more on data systems and sophisticated analytics in order to reduce uncertainty in decision-making. What has suffered, or at least been neglected, in this rush toward certitude and decisiveness is the more reflective conversation about purpose. It isn't that companies don't have mission statements; it is that they have tended to see them as decorations or hood ornaments rather than as an integral part of the engine of the company. An example of this was recently provided by McKeown (2012) when he began his *Harvard Business Review* blog with a game: "Below are three mission statements from three Fortune 500 companies. Try to match each company with its mission statement." One mission statement read, "Profitable growth through superior customer services, innovation, quality and commitment," while another stated, "To be the leader in every market we serve, to the benefit of our customers and our shareholders." Clearly, the exercise was a game of chance since, as he noted, the largely indistinguishable statements make the task almost impossible.

Contrast this with the idea of mission-driven organizations. Such entities are formed and managed to accomplish goals that extend beyond profits for stakeholders and owners to include other benefits. That does not mean mission-driven organizations are solely nonprofit. They can be for-profit or nonprofit, public or private, governmental or nongovernmental, philanthropic or religious. The result is an interesting twist. For nonprofits, mission is the same as profits for private sector companies. The bottom line for the American Red Cross is hardly a simple financial metric: "The American Red Cross prevents and alleviates human suffering in the face of emergencies by mobilizing the power of volunteers and the generosity of donors."

But over the last decade or so we have also witnessed the rise of consumers who care as much about the companies from which they buy as they do about their products or services. In this environment, there is a value proposition that has been created for those companies that make an authentic commitment to higher-order goals that create an ethos of social good:

- "Build the best product, cause no unnecessary harm, use business to inspire and implement solutions to the environmental crisis."—Patagonia's mission statement
- "Our mission: to inspire and nurture the human spirit—one person, one cup and one neighborhood at a time."—Starbucks mission statement

Perhaps this new mission-driven philosophy is best summed up with a vivid example in the book *Purpose: The Starting Point of Great Companies*:

> Purpose is bigger than strategy. At best, strategy is . . .
> a step-by-step path toward optimal results. Enron had
> strategy—indeed, it had many strategies. But strategies are
> about means; they cannot be an end in themselves. An
> end is a reason. Enron lacked a reason—it lacked Purpose.
> (Mourkogiannis, 2006, p. 6)

## The Dual Mission of Community Colleges

The importance of mission to community colleges cannot be overstated. There are really two major reasons for this. The first reason is that community colleges are truly mission-driven organizations. The history of these institutions has been well documented from initial conceptualization at the turn of the 20th century as junior colleges serving as the first 2 years of a liberal arts higher education. That history includes a remarkable growth in enrollment and an equally remarkable expansion of mission from a narrow preparatory focus to a comprehensive purpose that is sweeping in its scope. At the core, however, since the very beginning, has been the promise of the open door. The idea that higher education should be available to all has been a uniquely successful American experiment as "nobly" stated in the introduction of *Minding the Dream:*

> America as we know it today would not exist without her community colleges. The inclusive, democratic, and meritocratic impulses of the community colleges, and the transparent boundaries between college, work, and social life, have kept alive a promise of advancement and opportunity unlike any other institution in the United States. (Mellow & Heelan, 2008, p. xiii)

If the American community college is not the quintessential mission-driven organization, it is hard to imagine an organization with a more earnest desire for achievement.

While open access has remained a steadfast belief, it is also closely coupled with another foundational purpose of intense community involvement. Gleazer (1980) expressed the idea that a primary element of the community college mission is "to encourage and facilitate lifelong learning with community as process and product." A major report from the then American Association of Community and Junior Colleges titled *Building Communities: A Vision for a New Century* expanded on this central idea:

> Building communities is . . . an especially appropriate objective for the community college because it embraces the institution's comprehensive mission . . . . The building of community, in its broadest and best sense, encompasses a concern for the whole, for integration and collaboration, for openness and integrity, for inclusiveness and self-renewal. (Commission on the Future of Community Colleges, 1988, p. 62)

But while open access and community building have remained steadfast beliefs, what has changed has been a slowly evolving set of stakeholder expectations and the challenge associated with multiple, and in some cases competing, missions. Over the intervening 25-year period, the comprehensive mission of transfer, career preparation, basic skills and developmental education, continuing education and community service, and access has been pushed and pulled in numerous directions. Many aspects of these skirmishes have been well documented in *Community College Missions in the 21st Century* (Townsend & Dougherty, 2006). The authors noted that the most prevalent debate is the issue of general education and transfer versus workforce development. The term *versus* is used intentionally here because the debate has often been couched in this manner; that is, an emphasis on one mission is by definition a diminishment of the other. Another discussion that follows the same path is the increasing number of community colleges offering honors programs and whether such programmatic choices come at the expense of the open access obligation. The amount of resources devoted to noncredit and lifelong learning has been seen through a similar lens that suggests that those very same resources come at a cost to credit programs.

The second reason that mission and mission statements are critical to any discussion of community colleges is regional accreditation. An analysis of the six regional accreditation agencies (see Table 2.1) results in a very consistent finding. Across all accrediting agencies there is specific and substantive attention paid to the role of mission in the standards used to evaluate community colleges. In particular, many of the standards want the institutions to provide information on who the institution serves and its intended student population. They often also want the colleges to describe how the mission is used to guide operations and give direction to activities—programs and practices. Most importantly, the stated mission of the institution is the very first criterion or standard in each of the regional accrediting agencies. This fact alone reinforces the notion of the inherent mission-driven nature of American community colleges.

For community colleges, then, the bottom line is that mission and mission statements have a dual role. First, as an enumeration of the purpose of the institution, they should play a key role in describing a destination worth working hard to achieve. And by doing so, we mind the dream. Second, our accreditors have made it very clear that while having a dream may be optional, having a carefully enumerated mission statement that meets a set of strict criteria is not negotiable.

## Table 2.1 Mission-Related Accreditation Standards

| Accreditor | Standard |
|---|---|
| Higher Learning Commission: A Commission of the North Central Association | **Mission** <br> The institution's mission is clear and articulated publicly; it guides the institution's operations. Core Components: The institution's mission is broadly understood within the institution and guides its operations; The mission is articulated publicly; The institution understands the relationship between its mission and the diversity of society; The institution's mission demonstrates commitment to the public good. |
| Middle States Commission on Higher Education | **Mission and Goals** <br> The institution's mission clearly defines its purpose within the context of higher education and indicates who the institution serves and what it intends to accomplish. The institution's stated goals, consistent with the aspirations and expectations of higher education, clearly specify how the institution will fulfill its mission. The mission and goals are developed and recognized by the institution with the participation of its members and its governing body and are used to develop and shape its programs and practices and to evaluate its effectiveness. |
| New England Association of Schools and Colleges Commission on Institutions of Higher Education | **Mission and Purposes** <br> The institution's mission and purposes are appropriate to higher education, consistent with its charter or other operating authority, and implemented in a manner that complies with the Standards of the Commission on Institutions of Higher Education. The institution's mission gives direction to its activities and provides a basis for the assessment and enhancement of the institution's effectiveness. |
| Northwest Commission on Colleges and Universities | **Mission, Core Themes, and Expectations** <br> The institution articulates its purpose in a mission statement, and identifies core themes that comprise essential elements of that mission. In an examination of its purpose, characteristics, and expectations, the institution defines the parameters for mission fulfillment. Guided by that definition, it identifies an acceptable threshold or extent of mission fulfillment. |

| Table 2.1 Mission-Related Accreditation Standards (cont'd) | |
| --- | --- |
| **Accreditor** | **Standard** |
| Southern Association of Colleges and Schools: Commission on Colleges | **Institutional Mission, Governance, and Effectiveness** <br> The mission statement is current and comprehensive, accurately guides the institution's operations, is periodically reviewed and updated, is approved by the governing board, and is communicated to the institution's constituencies. |
| Western Association of Schools and Colleges: Accrediting Commission for Community and Junior Colleges | **Institutional Mission and Effectiveness** <br> The institution demonstrates strong commitment to a mission that emphasizes achievement of student learning and to communicating the mission internally and externally. Mission: The institution has a statement of mission that defines the institution's broad educational purposes, its intended student population, and its commitment to achieving student learning. |

We could stop here. But the last several years have fundamentally challenged everything. A series of environmental trends—an economic recession, transformative technologies, demographic shifts, and political schisms—have created a vexing set of conditions that seem to have coalesced around a single, assumption-jarring issue. The American Association of Community Colleges (AACC) shined a bright light on the topic in a policy brief, *Rebalancing the Mission: The Community College Completion Challenge:*

> In a remarkable confluence, federal and state governments and foundations are urging a paradigm shift for community colleges and similar institutions, from one emphasizing access to one emphasizing completion. Because of the egalitarian philosophy guiding community colleges, this shift has complex and challenging implications. (Mullin, 2010, p. 4)

In the following year, the summer of 2011, AACC launched a new 21st-century initiative. After an extended listening tour, the 21st-Century Commission on the Future of Community Colleges was formed to synthesize the collected data and then was charged with the daunting task to, "safeguard the fundamental mission of the community college—ensuring that millions of diverse and often underserved students attain a high-quality college education—and to challenge community colleges to imagine a new future for themselves." The resulting document, *Reclaiming the American Dream: Community Colleges and the Nation's Future* (AACC, 2012) begins, in its own words, with "harsh judgments" on employment preparation that is inadequately connected to the job market, major disconnects in the transition between high schools, and baccalaureate institutions and … unacceptably low student success rates. The ambitious responses to these judgments are described in seven recommendations as part of Three *Rs*: *redesign* students' educational experiences, *reinvent* institutional roles, and *reset* the system to create incentives for students and institutional success. But, perhaps most importantly, at the very core of the exercise is the realization that "Community colleges must reimagine their purposes and practices in order to meet the demands of the future." The game has changed.

## Findings on Community College Mission Statements

As noted, all colleges in the sample I studied had a mission statement. Indeed, that was the starting point or minimum requirement for inclusion. Some institutions used the term *mission* as almost a category heading on their website, with values and a vision tucked underneath. The longest mission statement came in at 426 words. The shortest was offered by William Rainey Harper College, which proclaimed to have "the world's most succinct mission." They could be right. It was one word—"Finish." Other institutions that leaned to the more parsimonious were Fullerton College's "We prepare students to be successful learners" and National Park Community College's "Learning is our focus; student success is our goal."

This range really illustrates the challenge associated with conducting a critical examination of this initial element. In addition to some mission statements being quite short and others quite long, the level of complexity varied greatly based upon an institution's idea of what should be included (and by definition what should be left out). So, how to proceed? One organizing scheme can be created by returning to Table 2.1 and analyzing the mission-related standards described by the regional accrediting agencies. How do they define the parameters and components of the mission imperative? The following is the result of that analysis ranked according to how often the component was mentioned across the accreditors:

- What does the institution intend to accomplish?
- How does the institution communicate its purpose?
- How does the institution evaluate the fulfillment of its mission?
- How does the institution develop and update its mission?
- Who does the institution serve?
- How does the institution intend to fulfill its mission?
- What is the institution's stated goals?

Beginning at the top of the list, all six accrediting agencies contained language that related to the classic definition of mission. And, in turn, the overwhelming majority of mission statements contained language to the effect. The dominating twin terms used to describe a stated purpose were *opportunity* and *learning*. Creating or providing opportunity, as seen in the mission statements of Atlantic Cape Community College, Ridgewater College, and Alvin Community College, is at the forefront of how many community colleges see their purpose:

- "Atlantic Cape Community College creates opportunity by providing access to superior educational programs."
- "Ridgewater provides quality educational opportunities for diverse student learners in an inclusive, supportive, and accessible environment."
- "The mission of Alvin Community College is to improve lives by providing affordable, accessible and innovative educational opportunities to those it serves."

Learning, in its various forms, is also prevalent throughout the mission statements, as is seen with Anne Arundel Community College, Salt Lake Community College, and Mitchell Community College:

- "With learning as its central mission, Anne Arundel Community College responds to the needs of a diverse community by offering high quality, affordable, and accessible learning opportunities and is accountable to its stakeholders."
- "Salt Lake Community College is a public, open-access, comprehensive community college committed to serving the broader community. Its mission is to provide quality higher education and lifelong learning to people of diverse cultures, abilities, and ages, and to serve the needs of community and government agencies, business, industry and other employers."
- "Mitchell Community College, a learning-centered institution, provides affordable, high-quality educational and training programs and services to meet the changing and diverse lifelong learning needs of a multi-culturally diverse citizenry who live and work in a global society."

This is, of course, both predictable and appropriate. The American community college is a place where providing the opportunity to learn is seen as its driving force, its raison d'être. One other term was often used in mission statements. If "opportunity to learn" is the cause, then "quality of life" may well be seen as the effect as noted by Westmoreland County Community College and San Jacinto College:

- "WCCC improves the quality of life of everyone we touch through education, training and cultural enrichment."
- "San Jacinto College's mission is to ensure student success, create seamless transitions, and enrich the quality of life in the communities we serve."

The second component derived from Table 2.1 is the importance of communicating the mission to various stakeholders. Some accreditors made specific reference to this idea, and it aligns with earlier statements about mission-driven organizations—that is, people choosing to be affiliated with organizations because of what they stand for as much as the products and services they offer. Obviously, enriching quality of life and meeting lifelong learning needs are ideas that should to be communicated in an enthusiastic way. But the mission statements themselves in the data set provide little evidence of how that might occur. The term *communicate* appeared only nine times in a word frequency analysis and then it was usually associated with a student learning outcome. Moreover, my earlier observation about the lack of visibility associated with all elements of colleges' ambition on websites is reflected again here. The only conclusion that can be reached is that communication is not a well-developed part of the mission of individual community colleges.

The next component—evaluating the effectiveness of the mission—is equally problematic. The mission statements themselves don't offer much evidence to support how this might be done. There is one exception. The inclusion of specific language in the mission that refers to "institutional effectiveness," "continuous improvement," or "culture of evidence" suggests that the institution is interested in developing feedback systems to learn and grow. Such language, while sparse, was embedded in some institutions' mission materials:

- Coahoma Community College: "Ensure institutional effectiveness by planning, assessing, and evaluating all activities and programs."
- Sinclair Community College: "Manage our human physical and financial resources in a caring, ethical, and prudent way that facilitates a working and learning environment focused on continuous improvement."
- Passaic County Community College: "Through a culture of evidence and inquiry, the College is an effective steward of its physical, financial, and intellectual resources."

Next, several accreditors expressed specific interest in how a mission statement is developed, reviewed, and updated. This, of course, is the process question. It suggests that a mission needs to be both credible and dynamic. Some institutions include a footnote under their mission, vision, and values statements that state when the board reviewed and approved the documents. This sends a message that there is a evaluative cycle in place. Quite a few more are intentional about including the mission statement in the strategic plan but also including a section on methodology—that is, how the strategic plan, including mission, actions items, and so, was developed. Such efforts usually describe who was involved, the events, the timeline, and other descriptions that give stakeholder confidence that the process of developing the mission statement was both transparent and inclusive. A good example of this cyclical, evaluative mindset is seen at Fox Valley Technical College:

> The FVTC Strategic Planning Process is on a three- to five-year cycle. Key steps in the process include revisiting the statutory purposes of the College and reestablishing or revising the foundation statements—mission, vision, values—before developing strategy.

The fifth component centers on the important idea of who the institution serves. This idea is fundamental to the seminal question—"Why do we exist?" In some form, the purpose of any institution must be linked to constituent groups that provide the human and financial capital which, in turn, is converted into student learning and other outcomes. Table 2.2 shows a word frequency analysis for terms associated with the service component. The word *community* used alone is the dominant term used in mission statements to describe the service area and stakeholders. This is, of course, expected. An analysis of how the term is used, however, shows that while it is usually used in the sense of building communities, as discussed earlier in this chapter, it is also used to describe the internal environment (see Table 2.3).

### Table 2.2: Usage of Words in Mission Statements Denoting Service Area and Stakeholders

| Words | Frequency |
|---|---|
| community | 220 |
| access(ible), open | 141 |
| diverse | 87 |
| affordable | 38 |

Extending the discussion of *community,* every discussion of community colleges and their missions, including Cohen and Brawer's (2008) classic work *The American Community College*, stresses "open access" to a "diverse" community with "affordable" tuition. This, of course, reflects the egalitarian notion of being democracy's colleges that foster economic and social equality. San Jose City College, Bunker Hill Community College, and Sinclair Community College are illustrations of institutions that reflect this powerful idea:

| Table 2.3: Usage of the Word *Community* in Mission Statements | | |
|---|---|---|
| needs of students and the | community | by providing accessible |
| commitment to regional economic and | community | development |
| prepare individuals in our | communities | for life and work |
| workforce development needs of the | communities | it serves |
| services that support a diverse | community | of learners |
| within a supportive | community | that encourages academic excellence |
| educational opportunities to a diverse | community | of learners |
| the college nurtures a | community | of lifelong learners |

- "The mission of San Jose City College is to effect social justice by providing open and equitable access to quality education and programs that both challenge and prepare individuals for successful careers and active participation in a diverse, global society."
- "The student body [at Bunker Hill Community College] reflects the diversity of the urban community and encouraging this diversity is an essential part of the College mission. The College seeks to become a national model for successfully incorporating the strengths of many cultures, ethnic backgrounds, age groups, and learning styles into the curricular and extracurricular life of the institution."
- "We [Sinclair Community College] help individuals turn dreams into achievable goals through accessible, high quality, affordable learning opportunities."

Some institutions are even more specific in terms of their service areas and their intended student population. Laney College provides an illustration of this geographic orientation:

> Laney College, located in downtown Oakland, California, is a diverse, urban community college committed to student learning. Our learner-centered college provides access to quality transfer and career-technical education, foundation skills and support services. These educational opportunities

respond to the cultural, economic, social, and workforce needs of the greater Bay Area and increase community partnerships and global awareness.

The next to last component involves mission fulfillment. This idea is not well developed by the accreditors. In contrast, the colleges themselves spend significant effort enumerating the types of degrees and certificates they offer. About one in four community colleges explicitly state in their mission statements the degrees and certificates in the same straightforward manner as Bossier Parish Community College:

> To achieve its mission of instruction and services, Bossier Parish Community College is committed to: Offering associate degree programs, one-and two-year occupational certificate programs and specialized career training.

Specific mission-fulfilling programs are quite a bit more complex. Cohen and Brawer organized much of *The American Community College* around the various curricular functions noted in each state's legislation: academic transfer preparation, vocational–technical education, continuing education, and developmental education. Table 2.4 shows the frequency of words used in mission statements that are associated with academic transfer preparation and vocational–technical education using the terms *transfer, general education,* and *baccalaureate* then *vocational, technical, career, occupational,* and *workforce.*

Since roughly three fifths of community college students in credit

| Table 2.4: Usage of Words in Mission Statements Denoting Academic Program Goals | |
| --- | --- |
| **Words** | **Frequency** |
| vocational, technical, career, occupational, workforce | 252 |
| continuing education, adult basic education, contract/corporate training, lifelong learning, personal enrichment | 155 |
| transfer, general education, baccalaureate | 127 |
| basic skills, developmental, remedial education | 49 |

programs are pursuing an occupational course of study, the data make sense. While there remains the ongoing tug and pull between interest in transfer and articulation and what Jacobs and Dougherty (2006) referred to as the "new vocationalism," these two primary functions appear to coexist in the straightforward enumeration of programs. Bishop State Community college, for example, states in part:

> Our Mission is to provide high-quality educational opportunities and services that are responsive to individual and community needs for the citizenry of Mobile and Washington counties at an affordable cost. The College utilizes traditional and distance learning to accomplish its mission. Bishop State Community College fulfills its mission by offering the following:

- **Transfer education** designed to prepare students at the freshman and sophomore levels for transfer to other colleges and universities.
- **General education courses** in the liberal arts and sciences to support all college degree programs.
- **Technical, vocational, occupational, and career education courses** that prepare students for immediate employment, retrain existing employees, and promote local and state economic stability and competitiveness.

The continuing education function is quite a bit more problematic. As Downey, Pusser, and Turner (2006) stated: "One of the least understood community college functions, continuing education, can be defined broadly as the range of programs and services that provide workforce training, adult basic education, academic transfer curricula, personal enrichment, and community outreach courses." Other definitions focus more on noncredit classes while other definitions include corporate training. Using the terms *adult basic education, continuing education, contract/corporate training, personal enrichment,* and *lifelong learning* results in a significant number of mentions in mission statements, with *lifelong learning* being the dominant term. Perhaps the most important observation in this area is that given that this is one of the least understood community college functions, the community colleges in the data set don't offer much help in defining any of these terms. From the example above, Bishop State Community College goes on to state, "Continuing education and personal enrichment opportunities that support lifelong learning and the civic, social, and cultural quality of life." While this may not be a robust description, most mission statements just list terms like those in Table 2.4. There is usually no real attempt to describe the function or define the intended student base.

The real disconnect here involves basic skills or remediation—that is, foundation skills that are necessary for students to succeed in college-level work. Cohen and Brawer cite remediation as one of the key curricular functions of community colleges, and estimates are consistent that more than 50% of students entering community colleges are placed in remedial classes. Complete College America recently highlighted the extent of the problem in a follow-up to its 2011 report, *Time is the Enemy*, with *Remediation: Higher Education's Bridge to Nowhere* (2012). It begins:

> The intentions were noble. It was hoped that remediation programs would be an academic bridge from poor high school preparation to college readiness—a grand idea inspired by our commitment to expand access to all who seek a college degree. . .Sadly, remediation has become instead higher education's "Bridge to Nowhere." This broken remedial bridge is travelled by some 1.7 million beginning students each year, most of whom will not reach their destination—graduation. It is estimated that states and students spent more than $3 billion on remedial courses last year with very little student success to show for it. (p. 2)

Remarkably, terms and language associated with this important function in community colleges falls well below the other programmatic offerings. It is almost as if by not mentioning it, the challenges associated with college readiness can be effectively ignored.

The final component is "What are the institution's stated goals?" About one in five institutions in my sample enumerated goals separately in two different forms. The first was a list of institutional goals that followed a more broadly stated mission. Such goals were clearly not strategic and not associated with a specific timeframe. Rather, they were institutionwide and meant to imply a more enduring quality. Illinois Valley Community College and Naugatuck Valley Community College reflect this approach:

Illinois Valley Community College Mission Statement
IVCC teaches those who seek and is enriched by those who learn.
College Goals

- Assist all students in identifying and achieving their educational and career goals.
- Promote the value of higher education.
- Grow and nurture all resources needed to provide quality programs and services.
- Promote understanding of diverse cultures and beliefs.
- Demonstrate IVCC's core values through an inclusive and collaborative environment.

Naugatuck Valley Community College offers quality, affordable education and training in response to evolving community needs by providing opportunities to individuals and organizations to develop their potential.
5 Goals (What we will aspire for)

- At NVCC, students achieve their goals
- NVCC faculty and staff make a difference—at the college, in the community, in their fields of study, and in the lives of students
- NVCC programs meet and beat industry standards
- NVCC is an engine of change within Waterbury and the broader community
- NVCC is an effective, performance-based institution

A second goal-directed approach took the form of institution-wide student learning outcomes. Morgan Community College, for example, describes five common student outcomes: communication, critical inquiry, intra/interpersonal responsibility, quantitative reasoning, and information literacy. Another institution, Chaffey College, describes a set of student core competencies: communication; critical thinking and information competency; community/global awareness and responsibility; and personal, academic, and career development. While these institutions are resolute in defining that "on completion of their course of studies, successful students should be able to . . .," they are truly in the minority. Even though the concept of assessment is a driving force in accreditation, it is mentioned in less than 5% of the community colleges' mission statements in the data set.

I also explored the question "To what degree have current issues found their way into mission statements?" The following is a series of issues or topics that are currently being discussed in some form in the popular press or among educators:

- Community colleges are often being referred to as economic engines by college officials, elected officials, and others.
- The completion agenda suggests that access without an equal focus on success at community colleges is just an empty promise.
- The impact of technology in society should be reflected in more innovative instruction and an associated set of student learning outcomes and as a way to increase community college efficiency.
- Community college students are part of an increasingly global society and need to be engaged in multicultural experiences.
- Distance and online education is seen as being particularly effective as a way to increase access in community colleges by providing students with increased scheduling flexibility.

| Table 2.5: Usage of Words in Mission Statements Relating to Current Issues ||
|---|---|
| **Words** | **Frequency** |
| economic, economic development | 87 |
| student success, completion | 76 |
| technology, technological | 57 |
| global | 43 |
| distance learning, online | 19 |
| dual enrollment, concurrent, high schools | 13 |

- The ability of high school students to accelerate their learning through dual enrollment at community colleges is seen as a positive option for many students.

Table 2.5 provides a word frequency analysis of these topics. Several of these results deserve some additional discussion. Earlier it was shown the extent to which open access is a dominant idea in the mission of American community colleges. Table 2.6 enumerates the different ways *access* is used among the individual community colleges in the data set.

| Table 2.6: Usage of the Word *Access* in Mission Statements | | |
|---|---|---|
| educational programs and services | access- | ible to our diverse citizenry |
| to improve lives by providing | access- | ible and innovative educational |
| yet affordable education in an | access- | ible and supportive environment |
| The college supports open | access | to post-secondary education |
| takes pride in providing open | access | education for associate degrees |
| educational opportunity that provides open | access | to quality learning opportunities |
| It affirms equal | access | to all aspects of the institution |
| offers affordable, equal | access | to higher education |
| communities it serves through equal | access | to quality occupational, transfer, |
| With commitment to the values of | access, | opportunity, student success, |
| commitment to expanded enrollment, | access, | equity, and diversity |
| cultural richness, collaboration, | access, | success, innovation |

But the question remains whether there is equal attention being paid to designing institutions that are laser-focused on successful completion. The answer is no. The contemporary language of success or completion has not kept pace with the traditional language of access. There are exceptions. Perhaps one of the best is the truly integrated approach demonstrated by Cascadia College:

- **We strive for a place where ...** Every individual is supported and engaged in lifelong learning. (Our vision)
- **We do this by ...** Transforming lives through integrated education in a learning-centered community. (Our mission)
- **We stand for ...** a caring community, pluralism & cultural richness, collaboration, access, success, innovation, environmental sustainability, global awareness, responsiveness, creativity (Our values)
- **We teach students how to ... think** creatively, critically, and reflectively; **learn** actively; **interact** in complex and diverse environments; **communicate** with clarity and originality. (Our learning outcomes)
- **We are committed to ...** increasing opportunities for academic-transfer education, strengthening collaborations to enhance professional-technical programs, being a national model for community college best practices, helping students complete their education. ("complete" meaning to transfer, earn a degree or certificate, find a job, or complete an educational goal.)

My final observation is on the topic of dual enrollment. The Community College Research Center (CCRC) released a study in 2012 titled *What We Know about Dual Enrollment?* According to the research, more than 70% of high schools offer dual enrollment opportunities. The study reports that dual enrollment participation is positively related to a wide range of college outcomes, including enrollment and persistence, greater credit accumulation, and higher GPAs. Moreover, the evidence suggests that dual enrollment is associated with greater than average gains for low-income, lower-achieving, and male students. Such data align perfectly with the noble ambition of advancing opportunities for social and economic equality. All of this and yet there is hardly a whisper in mission statements about our primary suppliers and partners in the delivery of dual enrollment . . . the high schools.

# Conclusion

It should be clear from the information provided in this chapter that community colleges have a huge advantage when it comes to articulating their ambitions, which, in turn, can create the necessary desired state (see Figure I.1 in the Introduction). That advantage is being mission-driven. These are institutions of hope that are profoundly democratic and uniquely focused on providing learning opportunities to a broad swath of society. The challenge is that a mission is a framework or context within which an organization's actions are formulated. That scope is extremely broad. It can include, as the analysis of mission-related accreditation standards suggest, up to seven components. So, what should an individual community college include in its mission statement?

Several useful ideas follow from the background materials and primary data analysis. Perhaps most important is the notion that community colleges need to focus on the process of developing, communicating, and then revisiting the purpose of their institutions. The topic is too important to leave to a quick judgment or a routine reaccreditation exercise. But in doing so, it is important to acknowledge the range of choices involved. Brevity can be emphasized, institutional goals can be described, or an inspiring and distinctive purpose can emerge from deep dialogue. The options are many. What is important is to be intentional about what domain you want your institution to cover. It is necessary to be explicit about what mission means in the context of the institution and then be meticulous about developing the language knowing that, for decision-making purposes, what is not included can be as important as what is included.

Another useful idea is to remember that mission statements should, in turn, be useful. That means that relevance is critical. As such, current topics that address real issues should be part of the mission conversation. Yes, mission statements are meant to be more durable than a strategy. But they also need to reflect what is important to stakeholders and provide a certain measure of currency that engages everyone in the act of describing a desired state.

A final observation is that all organizations tend to focus downstream. That is, they tend to want to talk about their products and services. They discuss what they want to provide. Community colleges would appear to be no exception. The bulk of the mission statements were dominated by the enumeration of degrees and programs, those tangible products that can be easily described. But as any organizational development person will tell you, if you want to improve the quality of your output, improve the quality of your input. Work upstream. Whether that involves increasing dual enrollment or reducing the need for remediation such that the goal of increased retention and graduation is achieved, the approach remains the same: keep working upstream.

# CHAPTER 3

## COMMUNITY COLLEGE VISION STATEMENTS

### Defining Vision

One of the more straightforward definitions of vision has been offered by Nanus (1992) in his classic book on visionary leadership: "A vision is a realistic, credible, attractive future for your organization." The future that is described in a vision statement cannot be fantasy. It must represent a genuine possibility. The credibility of the vision is often a function of process—it must have emerged from the hopes and aspirations of the individuals within the organization, not merely proclaimed from above. Finally, the vision needs to describe an appealing tomorrow, a better place, not just an extension of an acceptable today. According to Nanus, powerful and transforming visions tend to have special properties such as the following:

- They are appropriate for the organization and for the times.
- They set standards of excellence and reflect high ideals.
- They clarify purpose and direction.
- They provide enthusiasm and encourage commitment.
- They are well articulated and easily understood.
- They reflect the uniqueness of the organization and what it is able to achieve.
- They are ambitious. (pp. 28–29)

Nanus and other leadership experts such as Warren Bennis (2003) go well beyond defining terms and describing properties. Nonetheless, the beginning point for them is simple: Vision is the key to leadership. Most of their effort is then devoted to a long list of tasks such as understanding current conditions, building scenarios, synthesizing information, choosing among options, and then translating vision into reality. Such is the work of leaders.

A different perspective has been offered by Peter Senge (2006). He conceives the process of "building shared vision" as being one of the five disciplines of a learning organization along with systems thinking, personal mastery, mental models, and team learning. The emphasis, then, is not so much on the individual but on the institution and the capabilities that need to be developed organizationally in order to foster momentum. Underpinning this approach is the belief that individual efforts are not enough. Heroes are not enough. Instead, the idea of a powerful, shared vision is such an intrinsic force that it needs to be understood as an organic exercise, one that is broadly comprehended and carefully nurtured.

Two dynamics appear to be important when taking this expansive view. First, it is apparent that shared visions provide focus and direction. Organizations often exist as amorphous entities. There are divisions and units; there are work groups and teams. Each of these partitions of the whole can have their own rules and subcultures. Individuals within these partitions often work with their heads down as they attempt to meet short-term deadlines and individualized goals. A powerful vision that is shared can bring coherence to such diverse activities. As personal visions align with a shared perspective, randomness is replaced by purposefulness and, in some cases, discord is replaced by harmony.

In addition to focus and direction, a shared vision can also provide energy and force. People want to be part of something special. Yes, the extrinsic motivation associated with a title and a paycheck is important. But people want to have their spirits lifted. They want, at a very deep level, to be emotionally engaged by their work and to make a connection to something larger than themselves. This is where the excitement begins, when there is a force in people's hearts. It is something that cannot be mandated or directed. It also cannot be assigned as a duty in someone's job responsibilities. The result is institutional vigor, a sense of dynamism that transcends a finely crafted organizational chart or a comprehensive set of human resource policies. These dynamics—

focus and energy—work together. And the effect can be remarkable. As Senge observed, "Few, if any, forces in human affairs are as powerful as shared vision."

## Vision in the Higher Education Context

The same organizing schema—individual and institution—can be used to review some of the vision materials in higher education. Those books and articles that have concentrated on educational leadership have tended to speak to a list of qualities that leaders will need to navigate the turbulent waters of our times. In one list (Miller, 2010), the qualities of contemporary leaders need to have include humility, enthusiasm, charm, integrity, tenacity, and courage. In another (Skinner, 2010), the author states that each college will sort out its leadership needs according to its distinctive aspects of mission and location, as well as its circumstances. But the author goes on to say that these differences notwithstanding, there are qualities that are needed by all institutions: strategic resource management, accountability, entrepreneurship, collaboration, communication, stewardship, globalization, board relations, and so on.

Occasionally, this disaggregated approach to leadership is pushed to the side and a more future-focused approach emerges. For example, the following observation by Robert Greenleaf (cited in Calder, 2006) reflects the view expressed by Nanus and Bennis that "vision is the key to leadership:"

By answering one fundamental question—"What will success look like?—an educational institution has begun a process of defining its vision. It is undeniable that an institution will ever be greater than its dream; therefore, what is needed first and foremost is an articulated vision to propel an educational institution into a preferred future. Unguided by a powerful vision, educational leaders are more likely to falter and therefore must have a cogent vision for their institution, for it offers a tremendous competitive advantage over others that operate without one. (p. 1)

Another holistic perspective is offered by the Malcolm Baldrige Performance Excellence Program for Education (National Institute for

Standards and Technology, 2013). It, too, sees leadership and vision as being inextricably linked by placing Leadership first among its seven criteria and then devoting the second greatest weight, other than results, to the leadership criterion. It begins by asking, "How do your senior leaders lead?" and then proceeds to enumerate under a Mission, Vision, and Values section the following questions:

- How do senior leaders set your organization's vision and values?
- How do senior leaders deploy the vision and values through your leadership system; to the workforce; to key suppliers and partners; and to students, other customers, and other stakeholders, as appropriate?
- How do senior leaders' actions reflect a commitment to those values? (p. 7)

The other context for discussing visioning in higher education is the institution or organization. I developed a performance improvement framework based upon the same systems thinking used by Senge and others. The major components of his operational model include process design and management, enablers, feedback, and personal involvement. But these interactive components are driven by another formative one—direction setting. Without an aim, we wander. We lose sight of what is important. Our decisions are reactive, and we spend inordinate amounts of time and scarce resources on insignificant issues or traveling down blind alleys. The rationale for this entire performance improvement framework is based upon the simple notion of, again, a focus that also provides energy:

There needs to be a methodology that teases out simple truths and sharply defined aims. Such a methodology must engage people in a dialogue to nail down what is truly important and fashion a riveting, compelling, and widely shared vision of what tomorrow can be. We need to begin with an aim—a true north—that becomes the driving force for all we do. (Seymour, 1995, p. 13)

Beyond this early effort to develop the use of visions and vision statement to drive performance improvement in an integrated, comprehensive fashion, the dialogue has been limited. The mission of community colleges, as discussed earlier, is broadly discussed and debated both in academic journals and in the popular press. Driving that debate is purely a matter of math: With almost half of all undergraduate students attending community colleges, it is reasonable that questions surrounding purpose should be discussed in great detail in a wide array of forums. There is also reason to believe that conversations about mission are being held on individual campuses. Indeed, the accreditation standards discussed in chapter 2 made it obvious that it would be difficult for a community college to avoid—even if it is only once in an accreditation cycle—a discussion of mission. But vision is different. Even though mission and vision are often co-located in a conversation and even used interchangeably at times, the fact is that mission has a certain regulatory heft that vision does not. The vision conversation, unlike the mission conversation, can be avoided . . . and it often is. One reason for this is that we can be completely clear about our purpose or mission, and yet be in complete disagreement about our vision for the future.

There is an exception. Much of the work on strategic planning in higher education has been led by the National Association of College and University Business Officers (NACUBO) with the development of a strategic direction being a core element. In *Strategic Planning in Higher Education* (Tromp & Ruben, 2010), for example, a seven-stage framework is developed beginning with mission, vision, and values (Phase 1) as a means to establishing organizational identity. Another NACUBO workbook, *Collaborative Strategic Planning in Higher Education* (Sanaghan, 2009), provides further support by describing how to conduct a vision conference that "brings together internal and external stakeholders to create a shared picture of the future." At least, then, within the context of strategic planning, there has been some focused dialogue about what the future at a community college should be.

## Findings on Vision Statements

Of the 226 community colleges that had a mission statement online, 167 also had a stated vision (74%). This is an important finding. The vision "What do we want to create?" is an essential element in creating the kind of structural tension that seeks resolution and drives focused action. While accrediting agencies do not mandate the articulation of a vision, the lack of one might suggest another question: "Do you not know what you want to create?"

Word frequency analysis suggests another issue. Vision statements really are about the future. As we might expect, then, the words *will be* are used in many statements in the manner shown in Table 3.1. Moreover, synonyms such as *aspires, envisions,* and *seeks* are also used to connote that the institutions are engaged in a journey, an active attempt to describe a future state. A total of 98 of the 167 institutions (or 58%), then, could have the effect of creating the kind of tension that results in nonequilibrium leading, in turn, to structural advancement.

| Table 3.1: Usage of the Words *Will Be* in Vision Statements | | |
|---|---|---|
| We | will be | the opportunity institution for every |
| worlds of opportunity | will be | the bridge into that future |
| prepare individuals in our | will be | for life and work |
| Bishop State Community College | will be | a comprehensive learning institution |
| Atlantic Cape Community College | will be | the region's preferred choice |
| Cecil College | will be | the premier provider for learning |

In contrast, another set of terms is used to describe institutions in the present tense, as is shown in Table 3.2. These statements suggest that there is no daylight between the actual state and the desired state. There is no need to resolve tension—moving on a new path of least resistance—when no tension has been created. This analysis suggests that, of the more than 200 community colleges studied, only a minority (43%) had forward-leaning visions that seek to inspire stakeholders and engage them in a collective action that moves the institution in a positive, meaningful direction. The majority of institutions either don't have a stated vision or the vision sounds a bit more self-indulgent—"is" being the equivalent of saying "we're already pretty good" or "will continue" suggesting that "we don't really have a destination but we will continue on the journey."

| Table 3.2: Usage of the Words *Is* and *Will Continue* in Vision Statements | | |
|---|---|---|
| ABC College | is | a learning-centered institution |
| DEF College | is | the leading force of educational |
| GHI College | is | recognized as the center of educational |
| JKL College | is | the college of choice and a model |
| MNO College | will continue | to be a leading edge community |
| PQR College | will continue | to be an active partner in building |
| STU College | will continue | to be the premier provider of world- |
| VWX College | will continue | to be a state, national, and global |

A second set of analyses center around the idea described in the beginning of this chapter of a successful vision needing to be "compelling and shared." Something that is "compelling" is convincing, decisive, and persuasive. It evokes an emotional response. Since it is unreasonable to think that all ideas or concepts are compelling, it follows that those that are persuasive or convincing are unique in some manner or form. One way to look at a vision statement, then, would be to see to what degree it differentiates one college from another. Does it help describe how your college is special? Unfortunately, a significant number of visions were unconvincing or indecisive at differentiating themselves. For example, "ABC College will be a dynamic educational leader exemplifying innovation and excellence within a student-centered learning environment." Table 3.3 shows other illustrations of the jargon-filled tendencies of some institutions.

There are two aspects of these statements that should be of concern. The first and most obvious observation is that the visions are virtually interchangeable. A simple cut-and-paste exercise could be used to exchange the name of one college for another, and there is little evidence to suggest that anyone would notice. The language does not enable any of the institutions mentioned to make the case for their being special. A second, but less overt, observation is that many institutions tend to use words like *excellence* or *quality* to describe themselves (see Table 3.4). Again, because of the almost mechanical use of these descriptors, they tend to be unpersuasive in conveying any real sense of distinctiveness.

## Table 3.3: Examples of Undifferentiated Vision Statements

DEF College is a dynamic, diverse environment where all are encouraged to become responsible community members, leaders, and world citizens.

GHI College is committed to excellence in instructional programs, student services, service to community, and leadership in economic development and cultural enrichment in the region.

JKL College will continue to enhance its standing as an exceptional college by striving for excellence in all its programs, services, and activities

MNO College will be a dynamic institution noted for academic excellence, accessibility, innovation, and service to students and the community.

PQR College will be the College of choice for successful student learning, caring student services and open access. We, the employees, will work together to create an environment that emphasizes people, respect, integrity, diversity and excellence. Our College will be a leader in demonstrating accountability to our community.

STU College will have the resources, programs, and services necessary to offer every citizen in its service region opportunities for learning. Students will build on their strengths and excel in the College's dynamic learning environment.

VWX College will continue to be an active partner in building and maintaining the academic excellence and economic vitality of the diverse communities it serves.

## Table 3.4: Usage of the Words *Excellence* and *Quality* in Vision Statements

| encourages an expectation of | excellence | in all we do |
|---|---|---|
| international recognition for enduring | excellence | as a comprehensive |
| innovation, collaboration, and | excellence | in educational programs and services |
| the offer quality education, | excellence | in student support |
| commitment to teaching and learning | excellence | within a supportive environment |
| delivery of the highest | quality | education and career development |
| committed to providing the highest | quality | education in an environment |
| that continues to offer | quality | programs as an evolving model |
| distinction and recognition for the | quality | and effectiveness of the college |
| delivered by a | quality | faculty and staff |

Next, to what degree are the visions shared? In the Introduction I stated that institutions of higher education had a unique challenge: They are an assemblage of departments and disciplines that act in an uncoordinated fashion. The "pigeonholes" of colleges and universities align with independent thinking and entrepreneurial activities but don't necessarily help when it comes to acting strategically or in a collaborative fashion. It has already been noted that quite a few community colleges do not display mission, values, or vision statements on their websites and that of those that have a mission, one in four do not have a publicized vision statement. So, preliminary evidence would suggest that the idea of a "shared vision" could be problematic for community colleges. It is important to be reminded again that publishing or printing a vision is at the simple, low-end of the communications spectrum. Placing it on a website or in a catalogue is easy; creating posters or designing it into business cards is not too difficult either. The challenging part is how you communicate ideas in such a way that they "stick."

## *Six Principles for Making Ideas Stick*
In the book *Made to Stick* (Heath & Heath, 2007), the authors explore why some ideas survive and others die. They offer six principles that enhance the degree to which people remember and share thoughts. These principles—simplicity, unexpectedness, concreteness, credibility, emotions, and stories—offer an interesting way to organize and examine the vision statements that are included in my data set.

### 1. Simplicity
It is far easier to remember a simple, straightforward concept than one that has layers of complexity and density. Heath and Heath (2007) described the task as follows: "To strip an idea down to its core, we must be masters of exclusion. We must relentlessly prioritize." The two visions below illustrate simplicity. The notion of continuous improvement is embedded in much of the language of accreditation. But Harford Community College has found a way to say that in a unique and memorable manner. It is a simple statement that you could imagine people at Harford using on a daily basis to challenge assumptions and create positive, structural tension. While a vision of "Moving Mountains" would usually be seen as almost a tagline, the fact that the institution is

Mt. Hood Community College makes all the difference. Not only is the vision simple and obviously connected in a very visceral way to the institution, it also speaks directly and passionately to what the faculty and staff will do to ensure student success . . . they will move mountains.

> Harford Community College: "We aspire to make our great college even better."
> Mt. Hood Community College: "Moving Mountains."

## 2. Unexpectedness

In describing this principle, Heath and Heath succinctly stated that the trick is to "violate people's expectations." Using words such as *excellence* and *quality* become utterly pedestrian after a while. Any real meaning is lost. The idea of distinction is quickly muddled in a tumble of words. Houston Community College chose to describe its aspirations using a word not used by any other college: relevant. For a community college in a very large city, the idea of being perceived as vital or central to the area's success is both profound and pattern breaking. Again, excellence or quality were mentioned 81 times; relevant only once. In the case of Sierra College, the pattern breaking centers around the initial phrase "We will challenge ourselves and our community . . . " The institution is declaring, from the beginning, that "good enough is simply never going to be good enough" for them and the community they serve. It is a refreshing break from self-serving platitudes.

> "Houston Community College will be the most relevant community college in the country. We will be the opportunity institution for every student we serve—essential to our community's success."
> Sierra College: "We will challenge ourselves and our community to become fulfilled citizens in a global environment by contributing to and engaging in the thoughtful application of knowledge guided by respect for others and the world in which we live."

## 3. Concreteness

The basic idea here is that abstraction is the enemy of remembrance. Concepts that are presented in ways that can be interpreted differently are vulnerable to being misunderstood and, then, forgotten in the jangle and clatter of daily living. Experiments in human memory show that people are simply better at remembering concrete, easily visualized nouns (*bicycle* or *apple*) than abstract ones (*freedom* or *personality*). The language of Los Angeles City College's "urban oasis of learning" is decidedly concrete because it creates imagery—a place that is safe, a sanctuary that empowers students and faculty to move beyond the grind of daily life in a big city. You can almost see the palm tree-lined campus off in the distance. Clark State Community College aligns abstract words that abound in higher education—*opportunity, learning,* and *achievement*—with a real sense of barrier-busting by repeating the word *without* over and over again. That is speaking concretely and unambiguously—we will not be satisfied until *you* reach *your* goals.

"Los Angeles City College is an urban oasis of learning
that educates minds, opens hearts, and celebrates community. "
Clark State Community College: "Opportunity without
boundaries, learning without end, achievement without limits."

## 4. Credibility

Sticky ideas are believable. They must be presented with a sense of integrity and sincerity such that there is real meaning in the message. As an example, using the terms *excellence* and *quality* to describe yourself might be seen by many as being largely self-serving. In the case of both Heartland Community College and Wake Technical Community College, they have defined themselves in terms of their stakeholders. As a "community resource," the stakeholders decide whether expectations are being exceeded. Declaring ourselves to be excellent is one thing, asking others to make that judgment displays confidence that leads to greater authenticity.

Heartland Community College: "Heartland is an
adaptable and collaborative community resource, promoting life-long learning and exceptional community progress."
"At Wake Technical Community College, our vision is
a college that exceeds the expectations of our stakeholders
for effective lifelong education, training, and workforce development by providing world-class programs and services."

## 5. Emotions

This principle states that we are more likely to embrace and remember an idea if it evokes an emotional response. Credibility, like simplicity, counts for a lot. But for people to really invest in an idea and make it theirs, they need to care. Sinclair Community College's vision creates an emotional scenario by describing a very real problem that faces many if not most students—an uncharted or uncertain world. It then proposes a solution: Sinclair as a "bridge into that future." For Chief Dull Knife College, the emotion is in honoring its history by keeping a quote of the college's namesake alive. More than a century after his passing, the words of Dull Knife, the great chief to the Northern Cheyenne people, seem appropriate for the past, the present and the future: "We can no longer live the way we used to."

> Sinclair Community College: "Before us lie uncharted world of opportunity. Sinclair will be the bridge into that future, giving open access to opportunity, intellectual challenge and self-discovery for students with diverse needs."
>
> Chief Dull Knife College: "We can no longer live the way we used to. We cannot move around anymore the way we were brought up. We have to learn a new way of life. Let us ask for schools to be built in our country so that our children can go to these schools and learn this new way of life."

## 6. Stories

Organizations spend a lot of their time developing and communicating what is, in effect, propaganda. Whether it is internally focused training materials or an outward-facing website, the intention is to describe a point of view that aligns with goals. But the real power of ideas lies in their ability to promote storytelling. Stories are natural. West Shore Community College has chosen not to just place the words "Our Vision" at the top of a page and then move on. Instead, it tells a short story about "pursuing greatness." Naugatuck Valley Community College's vision provides a different type of storytelling. By eloquently stating that "our students are considered our most sacred trust and our finest asset," it empowers all its faculty, staff, and administrators to make the vision come alive by telling and retelling stories about heroic efforts taken to help students succeed at their institution.

West Shore Community College: "The **Vision Statement** is intended to create a mental image of our preferred future. Our current vision statement, which has been in place for more than five years, still describes a future that we prefer. It provides the inspiration to travel a journey that will never end—the pursuit of greatness. The concept of 'pursuing greatness' is extraordinarily empowering and liberating. It drives us toward the rest of our vision—assuring student success and serving our entire community. Our Vision remains the same: Our vision is to be one of America's premier community colleges, driven by a passion for assuring student success; serving our entire community, and pursuing greatness."

Naugatuck Valley Community College: "At NVCC, the word 'community' is central and our students are considered our most sacred trust and our finest asset. Collaboration within and outside the confines of our immediate surroundings defines our actions and is the base for the rich intellectual, educational, cultural and civic-minded experiences we provide our students."

## Conclusion

Every day, in more than a thousand mission-driven institutions of higher education, difficult decisions are being made. Many of those decisions involve the allocation of scarce resources that impact the lives of faculty and staff as well as millions of students. If the heritage and headlines are true, these same enterprises have a direct and beneficial impact on both our economy and society equality.

The initial, short review of the concept of vision was unambiguous: Many organizations seek to catalyze the enormous potential of their human capital around a realistic, credible, and attractive future. Indeed, Peter Senge's quote is worth repeating here—"Few, if any, forces in human affairs are as powerful as shared vision." Against this backdrop of energy and vigor was a different reality being presented about the role of vision and vision statements in community colleges. The secondary research suggests that there is little emphasis or operational interest focused on "visioning" on individual college campuses. Yes, it is true that strategic planning almost dictates the development and publication of a vision statement along with a mission and an enumeration of values. But this almost appears mechanical or formulaic in nature.

The primary research reinforces this conclusion. Mission and vision statements are the principal element of what could be a college's stated ambition. At times, the question of "What do we want to create?" seems to get merged or subsumed under the mandated question of "Why do we exist?" Other times, the question doesn't appear to be asked at all. Moreover, the lack of differentiation and aspirational language in the statements that were studied suggests an equal lack of effort devoted to developing and crafting a narrative that describes an attractive future. A vision really does need to "stick" because of the powerful force it can provide if it aligns with people's personal vision. All of this suggests a largely unrealized potential. In a landscape littered with questions and doubt, in an environment filled with distractions and diversions, the ability of a community college to describe a compelling shared vision is a huge advantage.

# CHAPTER 4

## COMMUNITY COLLEGE VALUES STATEMENTS

### Principles Underlying Values

Everything we do, every attitude we hold, is based upon on our consciously or unconsciously held beliefs and values. Behind every decision is the same formula, an underlying structure that informs the choices we make as individuals. A quick review of lessons for personal change by Stephen Covey (2004) in *The 7 Habits of Highly Effective People* reveals a strong emphasis on a belief system. The first three habits (be proactive, begin with the end in mind, and put first things first) involve moving from dependence to independence (i.e., self-mastery). The next three (think win–win, seek first to understand, then to be understood, and synergize) have to do with interdependence (i.e., working with others). The last habit (sharpen the saw) relates to self-rejuvenation (i.e., self-renewal). The habits, then, are really a value system that seeks to enhance personal growth.

There is similar emphasis on values in the leadership literature. If leadership is the ability to influence others, then values-based leaders use words, actions and examples to inspire others to be highly effective. In a recent book, *From Values to Action,* Harry Kraemer (2011) enumerated the principles associated with values-based leadership. He suggests that such leaders are, first, self-reflective. The understanding of what matters most is largely an exercise of discovery. It requires a level of self-awareness that results in the setting of priorities. While external influences—books, experiences, dialogue—can influence this process, what is ultimately needed is an honest and earnest journey inward.

Another principle involves balance and perspective. By committing to balance a values-based leader is acknowledging that too much of anything is ultimately destructive. Appreciating different perspectives will ultimately provide the information required to maintain that equilibrium. True self-confidence is another principle. The core of this principle comes down to being comfortable with who you are. And a final principle is all about keeping leaders grounded—genuine humility.

When the unit of analysis shifts from the individual to the organization, values can be defined as the lasting beliefs or ideals shared by the members of a culture or organization. They describe what is good or bad and desirable or undesirable. As such, values can have major influences on an individual's attitude and behavior and serve as broad guidelines in an organizational setting. But organizational values must be understood in context. And that context is culture. Perhaps the best explanation of this idea is the conceptual hierarchy proposed by Schein (1985). He saw culture as being composed of three levels:

- Artifacts. Evidence of an institution's culture may be found in various observable forms—routine procedures, daily and periodic rituals, language, stories and myths—at this level.
- Values. The second level of culture is made up of widely shared beliefs or sentiments about the importance of certain goals, activities, relationships, and feelings.
- Basic assumptions and beliefs. The final level, understood to be the foundation of culture and unobservable, consists of the unstated and implicit assumptions that undergird both artifacts and values.

Numerous efforts have been made to expand on this and other similar conceptual frameworks that propose a variety of dimensions and attributes of organizational culture. If culture is the social glue binding an organization together, then much of the work has been to find specific ways to impact positively "how things work around here." Still, organizational culture is extremely broad. It comprises a complex, interrelated, and ambiguous set of factors. Out of this multifaceted stew, the dominant methodology for organizing and interpreting culture is the Competing Values Framework (Cameron & Quinn, 2011). The framework was developed initially from research conducted on the key indicators of effective organizations. The questions asked in the investigation were these: What are the main criteria for determining if an organization is effective? What key factors define organizational effectiveness? When people judge an organization to be effective, what indicators do they have in mind?

The resulting indicators of effectiveness were submitted to a statistical analysis, and two major dimensions emerged that organized into four main clusters. One dimension differentiates effectiveness criteria that emphasize flexibility, adaptability, and dynamism from criteria that emphasize stability, control, and order. The second dimension differentiates effectiveness criteria that emphasize organizational cohesion, consonance, and integration from criteria that emphasize an external orientation, differentiation, and independence. Together these two dimensions form four quadrants, each representing a unique set of organizational effectiveness indictors: Clan (Collaborate), Adhocracy (Create), Hierarchy (Control), and Market (Compete). As Cameron and Quinn concluded, "These indicators of effectiveness represent what people value about an organization's performance. They define what is seen as good and right and appropriate. The four clusters of criteria, in other words, define the core values on which judgments about organizations are made."

What is clear from this modest review is that, generally speaking, values play a significant role in the study of both effective individuals and organizations. From self-help to leadership to academic journals and popular business books, there is a strong emphasis on trying to understand the relationship between values as a core set of beliefs and effective organizations.

## Values in the Higher Education Context

The business enterprise, in many ways, has an advantage when discussing issues like values and culture over the higher education organizations. A business has a discrete set of bottom-line metrics beginning with profits and including market share and return on investment (ROI). Given that so much is at stake in a business's success, it makes sense that researchers, authors, consultants, and business executives spend inordinate amounts of time and energy trying to figure out the causal factors—"What can we do in our business to improve the bottom line?"

Higher education struggles with this means–ends dyad. Student learning and knowledge creation are the obvious bottom-line comparisons, but how we define those ideas and then operationalize the measures cannot be reduced to a glossary of accounting terms. Without the "ends" being clearly articulated, there is understandably much less emphasis devoted to understanding the "means."

The result is minimal attention to the study of values as a causal factor in organizational or institutional effectiveness in higher education. Instead, most of the consideration of values within higher education derives from a broader, more passive perspective on culture. The basis for this perspective was provided 25 years ago in a comprehensive review by Kuh and Whitt titled *The Invisible Tapestry: Culture in American Colleges and Universities* (1988). This exhaustive and enlightening work examines how cultural perspectives can be used to describe college and university life. As Kuh and Whitt stated, "Culture is viewed as an interpretive framework for understanding and appreciating events and actions in colleges and universities rather than as a mechanism to influence or control behavior." Much of their time is devoted to looking at the threads of institutional culture and features such as rituals and ceremonies. Artifacts like architecture are described. Various subcultures—faculty, disciplines, administrative—are explored in detail. A small slice of this cultural exposition is devoted to values. While referencing Burton Clark's (1984) work that suggested that four values (justice, competence, liberty, and loyalty) influence the academic enterprise, they concluded that

> Some institutional values are conscious and explicitly articulated; they serve a normative or moral function by guiding members' responses to situations. Most institutional values, however, are unconsciously expressed as themes (e.g., academic freedom, tradition of collegial governance) or are symbolic interpretations of reality that give meaning to social actions and establish standards for social behavior. (p. 23)

With this narrow exception, most of the research, writing, and focus in higher education, including community colleges, has been on describing the nature of the academic profession as an institutional subculture. For instance, there are the basic values of the pursuit and dissemination of knowledge, autonomy in the conduct of academic work, and collegiality or the idea of a community of scholars that provide mutual support. But the idea that we should be devoting time to "understanding and appreciating" the culture of these institutions, is, again, in sharp contrast to the work in organizations as described earlier where culture and values can and should be actively shaped to produce more effective outcomes.

An exception to this invisible tapestry is the very visible inclusion of values as part of strategic planning in higher education in the same context as mission and vision. As an example, when Tromp and Ruben (2010) worked through their strategic planning workbook, they listed a series of questions to help institutions reflect on what they value:

- What fundamental beliefs are prized within the institution, department, or program?
- Are these principles explicit or implicit?
- Does the understanding permeate the organization?
- How consistently are the value translated into the behavior of faculty and staff? How would you know if that were the case?
- In what ways are issues of integrity and ethics important in the day-to-day activities of your organization? (p. 49)

While much of the research and writing on culture and values in organizations is focused on identifying levers that impact performance, the same type of analyses in higher education is largely devoted to understanding the subcultures of academe as a sociological exercise. There does not seem to be much interest in exploring values as a predictive variable, something that can be used in a strategic fashion to advance the goals of the institution.

## Findings on Values Statements

As I have noted, of the 226 community colleges that had a mission statement, 167 also had a stated vision (74%). A smaller number, 148, had language that spoke to values or principles (65%). The concept of "important and enduring beliefs or ideals shared by members of a culture about what is good or desirable and what is not" is labeled different things by different institutions in the sample. Usually the term is *values* with a combination of various modifiers—e.g., *core values, shared values,* or *guiding values.* In addition, another set of terms are used to a much lesser degree to express the same meaning: *philosophy, (guiding) principles, (core) commitments, (core) themes,* and *beliefs.* The range of these statements, however they were described, was from short lists of five to seven values to a 742-word document that included a dozen values that were described in full detail. In reviewing the formatting and content associated with the values statements, I counted 35 institutions, or 24%, whose statements consisted of either just a list of words or a list with very short descriptions (see Table 4.1).

### Table 4.1: Examples of Values Statements Consisting of Short Lists

| ABC College | DEF College | GHI College | JKL College |
|---|---|---|---|
| • commitment<br>• community<br>• diversity<br>• excellence<br>• heritage<br>• hope<br>• innovation<br>• integrity<br>• leadership<br>• learning<br>• teaching | • diversity<br>• excellence<br>• innovation<br>• integrity<br>• knowledge<br>• respect<br>• teamwork | • engaged learning<br>• community service<br>• leadership<br>• innovation<br>• integrity<br>• entrepreneurship<br>• stewardship | • excellence in education and teaching<br>• student learning and scholarship<br>• innovation<br>• civility and integrity<br>• caring personalized service<br>• diversity<br>• accessibility<br>• quality environment<br>• community engagement |

| MNO College | PQR College | STU College | VWX College |
|---|---|---|---|
| • accessibility and sustainability<br>• student success<br>• effective teaching and learning<br>• community engagement | • student enrichment<br>• community advocacy<br>• shared leadership<br>• excellence | • student learning and development<br>• excellence and innovation<br>• educational access and diversity<br>• integrity, accountability and collaboration | • integrity<br>• accountability<br>• diversity<br>• teamwork<br>• creativity |

Most of the institutions in the sample went beyond merely listing a set of values (or a very short description) to include longer, more detailed descriptions. For example, instead of just listing the word *collaboration,* institutions would state, "Collaboration: Working together as colleagues on college issues and decisions and actively seeking to form partnerships with our community and other organizations to address mutual goals" or "Collaboration, by bringing together individual knowledge and talents, creates teams that are greater than the sum of their parts. Such teamwork maximizes benefits to individuals and the community." A small number of institutions in the sample forego the standard enumeration of a set of values and use prose to describe their belief system. Delaware Technical Community College attempts to synthesize individual values into a values statement that has one or more summative ideas such as "One College philosophy" and "getting it right":

> Delaware Technical Community College values the One College philosophy, our collective commitment by all employees to create a consistent student experience throughout the entire College, across all locations—an experience that reflects our proud legacy of providing Delawareans with access, opportunity, excellence, and hope to achieve their dreams through education. We believe that student success is paramount; that open, honest and respectful communications is essential, and that a strong sense of team spirit is the key to "getting it right" for the communities we serve.

I conducted a word frequency analysis on all value statements in order to understand broadly what exactly the institutions say they value. Table 4.2 shows the results. As might be expected, the most frequently used word was *student.* The majority of the time, however, the word was used in the context of all stakeholders—that is, faculty, staff, administrators, and students. *Community* was the second most frequently used word, sometimes as part of *community college,* but mostly to denote to the community that the college served. I then noted eight clusters of terms in descending order:

- Integrity: firm adherence to a code of especially moral or artistic values.

- Excellence: the quality of being excellent.
- Respect: high or special regard.
- Learning: knowledge or skill acquired by instruction or study.
- Innovation: the introduction of something new.
- Diversity: the inclusion of different types of people in a group or organization.
- Collaboration: to work jointly with others or together especially in an intellectual endeavor.
- Access: freedom or ability to obtain or make use of something.

### Table 4.2: *Values* Word Frequency Analysis

| Words | Frequency |
|---|---|
| student | 365 |
| community | 294 |
| integrity, honesty, trust, fairness | 289 |
| excellence, quality | 234 |
| respect, respectful | 163 |
| learning, lifelong learning | 156 |
| innovation, creativity, curiosity | 152 |
| diversity, inclusive | 131 |
| collaboration, teamwork | 118 |
| access, opportunity | 104 |
| responsibility | 79 |
| accountability | 70 |
| responsiveness | 39 |
| continuous improvement | 36 |
| sustainable, sustainability | 30 |
| stewardship | 28 |
| academic freedom, shared governance | 16 |
| transparent | 8 |

Looking with a more focused lens on values statements, there are a number of ways in which community colleges have been able to create some distinctiveness in their attempts to answer the question, "What do we believe?" This individuality has manifested itself in four different forms: emotion, reflection, connection, and action. The first form is to use language or style that is successful in evoking an emotional response. Words such as *commitment, embrace, stewardship,* and *responsibility* express a very personal sentiment as can be seen in Los Angeles Valley College's ten "Core Commitments," two of which are as follows:

- Innovation. We promote a climate of discovery that values and embraces inquiry, continuous improvement and welcome creative solutions as we seek new, flexible and responsive ways to fulfill our mission.
- Environmental Stewardship. We foster responsibility and pride in our campus and serve as a model of sustainability, being mindful of the impact we have on the environment, as individuals and as a community.

Similarly, Bishop State Community College refers to its 10 beliefs as "Principles of Integrity" and uses careful, well-defined language to describe its environment:

- Helpfulness: We help by providing beneficial knowledge information and training to individuals, groups and communities.
- Orderliness: We organize data, information, facts and ideas in a manner that is useful, retrievable and applicable.
- Betterment: We seek to be better every day in every facet of our work.
- Thrift and Value: We conscientiously accept the responsibility for stewardship of all funds, to use money wisely and faithfully.

The second way in which some community colleges have been able to describe values that resonate in a more unique way is by showing the extent to which they have reflected on the subject. There is a certain sincerity, a depth of consideration in what Carteret Community

College believes as evidenced by their opening statement and several of their stated values:

> At Carteret Community College, we believe our purpose is to serve the citizens of Carteret County. To fulfill this purpose, we further believe our greatest assets are the people we employ. We the employees of Carteret Community College, united by common purpose share these values:

- Learning. Learning for our students and for ourselves.
- Service. Service to our community and to each other. We help others.
- Integrity. Integrity in word and deed. We trust each other and are trustworthy.

West Virginia Northern Community College takes a similar path to distinctiveness. Rather than a sterile list of words, their values seem to emerge from the individuals themselves in the form of a "Pledge to Students" that includes the following:

> We, the faculty, staff and administrators of West Virginia Northern Community College, reaffirm our commitment to our common mission:

- As faculty, we are a community of scholars who place a top priority on teaching, learning and advising.
  As classified staff, we serve the students and the College by facilitating and enhancing the total educational process.
- As administrators, we provide leadership for the development of students, faculty and staff; and we accept the responsibility for quality and accountability to the total development of the Upper Ohio Valley.

A third form that arose from the data set involved the idea of establishing a close, personal connection to stakeholders. The uniqueness associated with involving others suggests that values are something that are used to impact relationships and not just a set of standalone tenets.

Harford Community College has six stated values, but what is memorable is the conscious attempt, as seen in the opening sentence and several examples, to create a profound sense of togetherness:

We at Harford Community College are accountable to our students, the community, and each other, and hold the following values to be fundamental:

- Lifelong Learning. We value lifelong learning as the foundation for a better life. We prepare our students to contribute to their community and the world as knowledgeable, creative problem solvers and critical thinkers. We believe that learning should be engaging, stimulating, and enjoyable.
- Service. We believe in helping others, and we provide a safe and supportive environment. We are accessible and responsive to our students, our community, and each other.

Onondaga College takes a direct approach by referring to its values as "Principles of Community." The college enumerates four such principles that are clearly meant to create a powerful bond. Several of the principles are as follows:

- Respecting the *dignity* and *diversity* of others is fundamental to the educational process, as well as the hallmark of citizen participation and interpersonal relationships. *Respect* knows no bounds whatever our differences in socioeconomic status, race, age, gender, sexual orientation, ability, ethnic heritage or religious conviction. *Therefore*, I will respect the dignity and diversity of all people.
- We each affect one another; we are *interdependent*. We are role models for each other. What happens to one affects us all. A community characterized by *civility* and decency brings out the best in each of us. *Therefore*, I am committed to act with the greatest compassion and deepest wisdom.

An action orientation is the final form in which some institutions have chosen to establish their individuality. Ultimately, values that are useful are values that are used. While they are recorded in a statement of philosophy or commitments for publication and communication, what is really important is whether they are lived. For example, Red Rocks Community College states that their list of five principles "define our values and guide us in our actions and decisions." Several of these principles—innovation and integrity—can be seen below in follow-up statements that connote movement and intentionality:

> Red Rocks Community College is:

- A committed business partner, responding to industry and community needs through **innovative** solutions.
- A model of **integrity**, supporting our mission with thoughtful and judicious decision making.

Chemeketa Community College offers another illustration of being explicit in its intention to live its values. The college begins by placing its values in the context of action and only then go on to describe a set of four values, two of which follow:

> Our actions affirm our values, the character of the college, and how we do our work.

- Diversity: We are a college community enriched by the diversity of our students, staff, and community members. Each individual and group has the potential to contribute in our learning environment. Each has dignity. To diminish the dignity of one is to diminish the dignity of us all.
- Innovate: We innovate through reflection, analysis, creativity, and bold ideas. We design quality instruction, programs, and services to prepare students to meet the changing needs of our communities in a global society.

## Conclusion

This final element of an institution's ambition plays a unique role. A mission statement serves both in regulatory and emotive capacity. It strikes deep and provides foundational evidence for all of an institution's stakeholder and agency affiliations. It is basic to the existence of the organization and frames its activities. The vision, in contrast, provides the emotional fuel to be strategic and engaged. While the mission validates, the vision energizes. It creates a picture of a desired future state. A statement of values or guiding principles is quite different. Values provide the moral compass in the journey from where we are to where we want to be, the connective tissue that joins our purpose with our hopes and dreams. They describe how the organization wants life to be lived on a day-to-day basis.

That is why the problem that was described at Main Street Community College in the Introduction—a general and shared certainty that values are important but with no understanding of what the institution's actual beliefs are—is so troubling. It is clear from the data presented that relatively little time is devoted to developing each community college's code of behavior. A list of words does not a value system make, let alone a value system lived. Ultimately, values don't have the advantage of being mandated by an accrediting agency like a mission statement, and they also don't have the single-mindedness of a compelling shared vision. All values do is help us commit to how we treat each other.

# CHAPTER 5

# ALIGNMENT OF MISSION, VISION, AND VALUES

## Resolution and Strategic Planning

I have spoken so far of three foundational elements of what has been referred to as ambition—the most important things that colleges seek after earnestly. While mission, vision, and values are at the core of what the institution is all about, their real significance is in the ability to catalyze resolution or a movement from the current state to a desired state by strategic intent. Briefly returning to the streets of Boston described in the Introduction, consider for a moment the decisions associated with building a new street. The previous street was simply constructed over an existing cow path. But what choices do we have when deciding how to extend the street? The path of least resistance would suggest that we identify where the cow path leads and then pave over it. The alternative is to describe a different ambition, one that explores motivations, aspirations, and beliefs. Obviously, that desired state needs to be an extraordinarily compelling destination. But if that description is powerful enough, it can create the kind of discrepancy vis-à-vis the status quo needed to identify a new way forward. But the next step is important, too. The road will need to be built.

When structural tension dominates an organization, the organization can advance. But will it? Strategic planning is the basis for resolution, since it is centered on developing a series of action steps, or means, to realize an end. Without the road and road map, the destination becomes more fantasy than a realistic undertaking and the path of least resistance—the cow paths—prevail.

Strategic planning, according to Bryson (1995), is "a disciplined effort to produce fundamental decisions and actions that shape and guide what an organization is, what it does, and why it does it." Moreover, strategic planning is an activity that can be used to set organizational priorities, focus energy and resources, strengthen operations, ensure that employees and other stakeholders are working toward common goals, establish agreement about intended outcomes/ results, and assess and alter an organization's direction in response to changing environmental influences.

The benefits of strategic planning are numerous (Bryson & Alston, 2011). They include the following:

- Increased effectiveness. The organization's performance improves and its mission advances. In addition, the organization responds effectively to changing circumstances.
- Increased efficiency. The same or even better results are achieved with fewer resources.
- Improved understanding and learning. The organization better understands itself and its situation, which can, in turn, guide future strategy development and implementation.
- Better decision making. A solid and coherent framework for decision-making is established.
- Enhanced organizational capabilities: Broadly based organizational leadership is improved, and the capacity for further strategic thinking and action is enriched.
- Improved communications and public relations. Mission, vision, values, goals, and strategies are communicated more effectively to key stakeholders.
- Increased political support. The organization's legitimacy is enhanced and supportive coalition created. (p. 4)

It is generally agreed that the important part of a strategic plan is not the plan itself but the planning process. It is the time and energy devoted to reflecting on purpose, the external environment, the internal capabilities, and so on that is so valuable. That reflection allows people to challenge existing ways of doing things and to then engage in different, more effective ways of doing things.

But one should not walk away from this brief synopsis with the impression that strategic planning is not without its critics or weaknesses. For example, Hamel and Prahalad (2005) have stated, "Although strategic planning is billed as a way of becoming more future oriented, most managers, when pressed, will admit that their strategic plans reveal more about today's problems than tomorrow's opportunities." This critique is largely based upon the belief by the authors that too much time and effort is usually devoted to extensive analysis of competitors' strength and weaknesses, of market niches and organizational resources, than in articulating a goal worthy of commitment. Others have focused on such areas as the "fallacy of predetermination," the concern that by enumerating future conditions we are attempting to predict what is inherently unpredictable or the "fallacy of formalization," the concern that the more elaborated the planning procedures become, the less dynamic and vibrant the plan becomes (Mintzberg, 1994).

More recently, a newer, more robust model of strategic planning has emerged in what is referred to as a "collective ambition" by Ready and Truelove (2011) in the *Harvard Business Review*. In the past, strategic planning has been seen as a comprehensive, integrated approach to allocating an organization's scarce resources. It was the broad context within which daily decisions were made. The collective ambition model creates an even broader and more integrated context. So, what elements does an organization's collective ambition comprise? The following seven are adapted from Ready and Truelove:

- Purpose: your organization's reason for being the core mission of the enterprise.
- Vision: the position or status your organization aspires to achieve within a reasonable time frame.
- Targets and milestones: the metrics you use to assess progress toward your vision.
- Strategic and operational priorities: the actions you do or do not take in pursuit of your vision.
- Brand promise: the commitments you make to stakeholders (customers, communities, investors, employees, regulators, and partners) concerning the experience the organization will provide.

- Core values: the guiding principles that dictate what you stand for as an organization, in good times and bad.
- Leader behaviors: how leaders act on a daily basis as they seek to implement the organization's vision and strategic priorities, strive to fulfill the brand promise, and live up to the values. (p. 5)

Strategy and strategic planning, therefore, is a combination of the ends (goals) for which the organization is striving and the means (actions) by which it is seeking to get there. One without the other is just rhetoric. It is only when they are tightly connected that oratory and wishful thinking are replaced by virtuous cycles of performance improvement.

## Strategic Planning in the Higher Education Context

The application of strategic planning principles to institutions of higher education has a defined genesis. In 1983, after years of surging growth at colleges, George Keller (1983) declared in his seminal book *Academic Strategy: The Management Revolution in American Higher Education*, "A specter is haunting higher education: the specter of decline and bankruptcy." Colleges were experiencing inflationary costs at the time as well as diminishing government support and declining enrollments. According to Keller, the only lasting solution was to view colleges as organizations and to take a more vigorous and targeted approach to management: "I believe strategic decision making is what nearly all colleges and universities will need to practice in the years ahead."

Over the next several decades, strategic planning became a defined part of the management of most colleges and universities in the country. The principles and practice of total quality management or continuous quality management with the emphasis on process and systems theory helped to expand many colleges' thinking. An even broader context has been developed by linking planning, budgeting, and institutional research in more comprehensive whole systems models and metaphors (Seymour, 2002, 2011). A specific example, as has been mentioned before, of this "thinking in wholes" approach can be seen in the Malcolm Baldrige National Quality Award's Education Criteria for Performance Excellence. Strategic planning is one of six process categories leading to results in a larger Performance Excellence Framework.

There have been critics along the way in higher education, too. Benjamin Ginsberg (2011), in his book on the fall of the faculty, sees a strong relationship between the ubiquity of planning at America's colleges and universities and the continuing growth of administrative power. He believes that strategic planning is an attempt by the senior administration to signal to the faculty, to the trustees, and to the general community that they are in charge. Moreover, the process of developing the plan is meant to co-opt participants while the plan itself is, according to Ginsberg, a "substitute for action."

In chapter 2, Table 2.1 enumerated how an institution's mission had become a specific requirement in every regional accreditor's criteria. Table 5.1 looks at the language associated with strategic planning by the six regional accreditors. What should be quickly evident from Table 5.1 is the inclusion of language that extends beyond strategic planning. Just as mission, vision, and values are a subset of strategic planning, it would appear that strategic planning is, in turn, a subset of institutional effectiveness. In a recent *New Directions for Community Colleges* monograph, Ronald Head (2011) attempted to trace the origins of institutional effectiveness in community colleges. He noted that the concept has evolved into an umbrella term that both has specific contexts and describes a process.

One context is assessment, usually used in terms of student learning and learning outcomes. A second is accreditation as various regional accrediting agencies began moving from being input-driven to outcomes-driven. The final context is accountability. Pressure to demonstrate effectiveness increased as external forces demanded that colleges and universities be held accountable for their product. Finally, largely due to the influence of accreditors, institutional effectiveness has evolved into a cyclical process linking institutional purpose with institutional improvement: purpose drives goals and objectives which are then evaluated and the results are used to inform the original purpose.

## Table 5.1 Accreditation Standards Related to Strategic Planning

| Accreditor | Standard |
|---|---|
| Higher Learning Commission: A Commission of the North Central Association | **Resources, Planning, and Institutional Effectiveness** <br> The institution's resources, structures, and processes are sufficient to fulfill its mission, improve the quality of its educational offerings, and respond to future challenges and opportunities. The institution plans for the future. |
| Middle States Commission on Higher Education | **Planning, Resource Allocation, and Institutional Renewal** <br> An institution conducts ongoing planning and resource allocation based on its mission and goals, develops objectives to achieve them, and utilizes the results of its assessment activities for institutional renewal. Implementation and subsequent evaluation of the success of the strategic plan and resource allocation support the development and change necessary to improve and to maintain institutional quality. |
| New England Association of Schools and Colleges Commission on Institutions of Higher Education | **Planning and Evaluation** <br> The institution undertakes planning and evaluation to accomplish and improve the achievement of its mission and purposes. It identifies its planning and evaluation priorities and pursues them effectively. |
| Northwest Commission on Colleges and Universities | **Planning and Implementation** <br> The institution engages in ongoing, participatory planning that provides direction for the institution and leads to the achievement of the intended outcomes of its programs and services, accomplishment of its core themes, and fulfillment of its mission. |
| Southern Association of Colleges and Schools: Commission on Colleges | **Institutional Effectiveness** <br> The institution engages in ongoing, integrated, and institution-wide research-based planning and evaluation processes that (1) incorporate a systematic review of institutional mission, goals, and outcomes; (2) result in continuing improvement in institutional quality; and (3) demonstrate the institution is effectively accomplishing its mission. |

| Accreditor | Standard |
|---|---|
| **Table 5.1 Accreditation Standards Related to Strategic Planning (cont'd)** | |
| Western Association of Schools and Colleges: Accrediting Commission for Community and Junior Colleges | **Institutional Mission and Effectiveness** The institution uses analyses of quantitative and qualitative data in an ongoing and systematic cycle of evaluation, integrated planning, implementation, and re-evaluation to verify and improve the effectiveness by which the mission is accomplished. |

As an example, the Southern Association of Colleges and Schools (SACS, 2012) has two categories of criteria—core requirements and comprehensive standards—with the core representing 12 items that are basic, broad-based, foundational requirements. The items are a threshold if you will. One of those 12 items is institutional effectiveness and is described as follows:

> The institution engages in ongoing, integrated, and institution-wide research-based planning and evaluation processes that (1) incorporate a systematic review of institutional mission, goals, and outcomes; (2) result in continuing improvement in institutional quality; and (3) demonstrate the institution is effectively accomplishing its mission. (p. 18)

The language and logic used by SACS and, to a lesser degree, the other regional accreditors, represents a systems perspective that focuses on the whole and not the parts. It links processes to outcomes and expects that feedback loops be overtly designed into the operations of the institution in order to fuel organizational learning and performance improvement.

## Findings on Alignment of Mission, Vision, and Values

As I noted in the first chapter, those institutions included in the data set had a defined mission statement. A subset of them also had vision and values statements on their respective websites. The content analyses described in the next three chapters were focused narrowly on those elements of the colleges' ambitions. The analysis in this chapter is less precise but still of critical importance. The research question here is, "To what degree are mission, vision, and values linked to the larger context of strategic planning or institutional effectiveness?" This is an important aspect of this critical examination because it explores whether the colleges have both created the necessary tension by describing forward-leaning ambitions and have aligned that tension with a bias for action or resolution.

The primary way in which this alignment might be done is as follows. First, it is reasonable to expect that mission, vision, and values would have some headline value—that is, they would deserve space as standalone items because of the questions they both ask and answer. A vision statement that responds to the question "What do we want to create?" should be featured in some way. But it is also true, as we have seen, that mission, vision, and values are the key drivers of a college's strategic plan. We expect, then, that they would also be featured in the plan itself. Finally, the broadest possible view of an institution would be some sort of systems model that describes how a collective ambition drove continuous improvement and institutional effectiveness.

Since the majority of information on mission, vision, and values was found under an About Us tab, the first part of the analysis was to see whether the college had a strategic plan on its website and whether it was co-located with mission, vision, and values. Using both the site map and a search function, if available, of the 226 institutions studied I found that only 26% or 59 had strategic plans posted online. Of those 59, only 41 had the strategic plan either on the same Web page with mission, vision, and values or with an identifiable link (18% of the total). I found that the majority of these 59 plans began with the specific delineation of the college's mission, vision, and values and described an environmental scan or enumerated a list of strategic actions to be taken over a proscribed period of time. Still, 15 of those plans made no references to any elements of a more robust ambition. The action items stood alone. Finally, I attempted to identify institutions that had taken the additional steps to describe the broader, more integrated model of institutional effectiveness. Such a general model of institutional effectiveness and continuous improvement is presented in Figure 5.1.

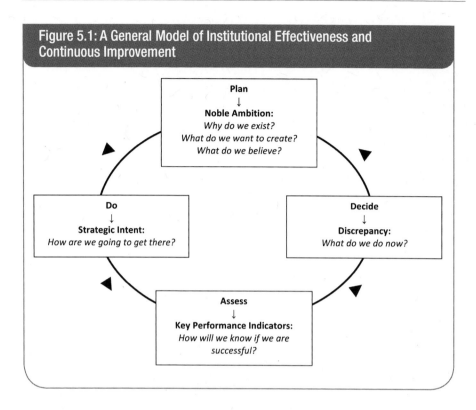

**Figure 5.1: A General Model of Institutional Effectiveness and Continuous Improvement**

The **Plan–Do–Assess–Decide** model is adapted to higher education from the commonly used Plan–Do–Check–Act cycle (also known as the Shewart Cycle). The **Plan** component is presented as the noble ambition associated with the three questions: Why do we exist? What do we want to create?, What do we believe? The structural tension produced because the desired state differs from the actual state is then resolved through the **Do** component—the development and implementation of a strategic intent that answers the question, "How are we going to get there?" The **Assess** component is really how we begin to extend the models presented in the Introduction by adding a critical follow-up evaluative question—"How will we know if we are successful?" These metrics can be specific to a gap analysis between the **Plan** and the **Do** or they can reflect a more broadly developed set of core indicators of effectiveness for community colleges such as persistence, student satisfaction, placement rates, and so on (Alfred, Shults, & Seybert, 2007).

The critical, closing-the-loop, component in the general model is **Decide.** Having generated the evaluative information, the question becomes "What do we do now?" If, for example, the strategic intent of the **Do** component has produced results in the **Assess** component that suggest that we have been successful, then the discrepancy between the actual state and desired state would necessarily have then been reduced. That is great in the short run, but in the long run something will need to change in order generate new, additional structural tension. In contrast, if the assessment suggests that the desired state has not been achieved, a whole new set of decisions about strategy will need to be made in order to seek resolution and structural advancement. And around and around the cycle goes.

There were only a handful of institutions that described this whole systems approach. Wake Technical Community College in Raleigh, North Carolina, was one. Under "About Wake Tech" is a page that includes Mission Statement, as well as Institutional Effectiveness, Accreditation, and Research. The mission statement link goes to a page with the mission statement, vision, and college goals. The institutional effectiveness link goes to a page that begins as follows:

Institutional Effectiveness is a cyclical process that involves the following steps:

- Establish meaningful goals
- Develop strategies to accomplish these goals
- Assess and evaluate the outcomes from these specific strategies
- Apply the knowledge gained from this process to improve tasks

The page includes a graphic model of the Annual Planning and Evaluation Cycle as well as the Wake Technical Community College Strategic Plan (2012–17). The plan, in turn, is fully integrated with a restatement of mission, vision, and core values along with goals and performance measures.

Another institution that described how mission, vision, and values are linked to a broader, strategic context is Fox Valley Technical

College. Along with their mission, vision, and values statement under About FVTC, the institution features Strategic Directions. One part of this Web page concisely describes the five directions—Learning Agility, Innovation Leader, Student Success, Robust Partnerships, and Cohesive Culture—while also linking to the 2011–14 Strategic Plan. That document begins with mission, vision, and values followed by the strategic directions followed by Strategic Plan Measures (baseline and target) for each of the five strategies. These measures answer another important institutional effectiveness question, "How will we know if we are successful?"

Fox Valley also has a corresponding document—Strategic Planning Process. It begins as follows: "The FVTC Strategic Planning Process is on a three- to five-year cycle. Key steps in the process include revisiting the statutory purposes of the college and reestablishing or revising the foundation statements—mission, vision, values—before developing strategy." It goes on to describe and graphically display a process that is based upon four questions: (1) Where are we now?, (2) Where do we want to go?, (3) How do we get there?, and (4) How will we monitor and measure results.

A final illustration of this comprehensive, integrated approach is provided by Houston Community College. Again, under an About HCC tab, the first header is Institutional Effectiveness. Included in that area of the page are the current and immediate past strategic plans as well as an annual report and an interactive dashboard that tracks nine measures including access, completions, and student engagement. An additional document—an Institutional Effectiveness Model—pulls all of it together.

The model is based upon two organizing principles. One is a reinforcing systems loop that links strategic planning loop (longer term) with an operations loop (annual). The idea is that as the top loop is successful in informing the bottom loop, the results generated operationally will inform and improve the ability to plan. The second organizing principle is Plan–Do–Assess–Decide stages built into the loops. For example, the **Plan** part of the top loop is mission, vision, and values followed by the **Do**—the strategic plan. On an annual basis the **Assess** stage includes the already mentioned annual report, dashboard, program review, and various college surveys. The final stage, **Decide,** states: "Stay the Course, Change the goal or the strategy, or Change both."

The important aspect of these illustrations is simply that mission, vision, and values are not perceived as separate elements that are part of a checklist of must haves. There appears to be a sincere attempt to link the ambition of the institution to strategic choices and then assess the impact of those choices moving forward in a dynamic and continuous fashion.

One of the more interesting findings as part of the critical examination occurred when I conducted what I call a "resolution" analysis. The methodology used to select the data set was convenience sampling within a set of strata—size and location. Still, the institutions were subsequently coded with a few other variables: whether they were Achieving the Dream leader colleges, whether they were finalists for the Aspen Prize in Community College Excellence, or whether they have members of North Central Association's alternative to standard accreditation—the Academic Quality Improvement Program (AQIP). There did not seem to be any correlation been the leader colleges and the Aspen Prize winners and an integrated approach. Of course, given the precise criteria being used to define success in both these situations, it is not necessarily surprising that there would not be any obvious alignment.

AQIP was the exception, though. The program, developed in 1999, is described in the Higher Learning Commission's (2007) *Introduction to AQIP* (2007).

> Based upon principles common to high performance organizations, AQIP draws from a variety of initiatives and programs—Total Quality Management (TQM), continuous improvement (CI), Six Sigma, ISO 9000 registration, state and national quality awards, and others. Many of AQIP's quality principles—focusing on key processes, basing decisions on data, decentralizing control, empowering faculty and staff to make the decisions that directly affect their work—have long been traditions in higher education, although their form and the breadth of their practice in particular institutions may vary greatly. Other components such as systems thinking and stakeholder focus appear at first to be new to academia, but turn out to be in close alignment with the values and behaviors of higher educators. (p.1)

What appears to be the key factor is both philosophical and procedural. While Table 5.1 illustrates the increasing use of institutional effectiveness language in regional accreditation, the basic approach is focused on a 5- to 10-year cycle. Once accreditation is granted, there is a natural lessening of focus and activity—that is, until the next report is due or cycle is initiated, which results in a flurry of intense activity leading up to the visit. AQIP is much different. It has three distinct cycles that occur simultaneously. The annual cycle requires the institution to tackle three or four action projects and then provide action plan Updates. A 4-year cycle requires the institution to create and maintain an up-to-date systems portfolio that describes key systems and processes the organization uses to generate its goals and performance results. Finally, the reaffirmation of the accreditation cycle is 7-year review of evidence from the action and strategy cycles. Fox Valley Technical College is an AQIP member as are 24 other institutions in the database (see Table 5.2).

## Table 5.2: AQIP Colleges

| # | College | # | College |
|---|---------|---|---------|
| 1 | Belmont College | 14 | Kaskaskia College |
| 2 | College of Dupage | 15 | Lakeshore Technical College |
| 3 | Columbus State Community College | 16 | Lamar Community College |
| 4 | Cuyahoga Community College | 17 | Montcalm Community College |
| 5 | Des Moines Area Community College | 18 | Morgan Community College |
| 6 | Dodge City Community College | 19 | North Hennepin Community College |
| 7 | Fox Valley Technical College | 20 | Red Rocks Community College |
| 8 | Garden City Community College | 21 | Ridgewater College |
| 9 | Grand Rapids Community College | 22 | San Juan College |
| 10 | Heartland Community College | 23 | Sinclair Community College |
| 11 | Hutchinson Community College | 24 | Southeast Arkansas College |
| 12 | Illinois Valley Community College | 25 | West Shore Community College |
| 13 | Inver Hills Community College | | |

Colleges such as Heartland Community College and North Hennepin Community College and others are strong illustrations of the kind of whole systems approach that appear to moderate the impact of institutional pigeonholing. All of the AQIP institutions in the sample have their systems portfolios featured prominently on their respective websites, giving real credence to another section titled "Exploring AQIP and Continuous Improvement" in *Introduction to AQIP*:

> Any organization interested in joining AQIP should first learn as much as possible about it and other quality improvement programs and stimulate a campus-wide discussion of how well participating might serve its needs and fit its culture. AQIP believes it is essential for any institution that is considering participation to fully understand the benefits and challenges of pursuing continuous improvement, and how much honesty and hard work the effort will require. An organization that currently has a flourishing quality program has already finished this first step. But if words like alignment, process, silo, team, and metric are foreign to campus discourse, the organization needs to encourage conversation and learn more about quality principles before continuing. It is critical that a core of people, including senior leaders, appreciates the principles of continuous quality improvement and the level of commitment required. Leaders need to clearly understand how system-wide continuous improvement can be introduced, how improved processes can be encouraged, and how enhanced performance can affect overall organizational fitness. (p. 5)

## Conclusion

I often use an automobile to illustrate a systems perspective. A car is a system. It has thousands of parts that interact to create a vehicle capable of rather impressive speed down a highway. Now picture an auto parts store. There are shelves upon shelves of radiators, drive shafts, and carburetors. Indeed, there are enough parts to make a few highway ready cars. But instead, what you have is a heap that isn't going anywhere. The difference between an auto parts store and an automobile is a function of relationships. In the former, the parts are independent; in the latter, the parts are connected.

Tension, as I have noted, creates a state of nonequilibrium. That is the promise of mission, vision, and values: Together, acting as a collective ambition, they can describe a desired state that makes it difficult to accept things as they are. But that is not enough. Hoping and wishing, dreaming and imagining, are insufficient by themselves. While most institutions in the sample have not connected the dots (or car parts), it is encouraging to see that there are exemplars (or high-performing cars) available. They have taken a systems approach. They actively and enthusiastically work to overcome the pigeonholing that is endemic to academic institutions or the disaggregation that is seen at the auto parts store. By doing so, it makes the task much easier. Viewed as a series of disparate parts, it is challenging to see the way forward. But once the pieces begin to align, once the aim is linked to the means, the promise of ambition can produce the necessary bias for action that leads to . . . resolution.

# CHAPTER 6

# RECOMMENDATIONS

This final chapter shifts gears. The primary motivation for moving forward on this endeavor was to produce something that could be put to use. I do so here by suggesting some promising practices that emerged from synthesizing the literature and the research findings presented so far. The nine recommendations are organized into three sets of three.

The first set reflects approaches that might be used as an institution begins to think about the manner and means of addressing its own ambitions. They are foundational and apply broadly to the other practices:

- **Embrace reflective practice.** Take the time to engage in deep dialogue and tackle important questions.
- **Make words matter.** Realize that language that energizes, differentiates, and is concise can help set the tone for defining a noble ambition.
- **Make process matter.** Know that processes that are transparent and inclusive will help create broad buy-in.

The next set of recommendations focuses on each individual element of an ambition—mission, vision, and values:

- **Be on a mission.** Live the mission; don't just write a mission statement.
- **Take the road less traveled.** Make sure your vision is distinctive and sets your institution apart from others.

- **Do what you say.** Do not state any values that you or other members of your institution are not willing to commit to every single day.

The final three recommendations are about execution. These are ideas that can advance the implementation of mission, vision, and values in meaningful ways:

- **Keep folding things in.** Align the elements of ambition with planning activities and daily decision making.
- **Never stop communicating.** Design an internal communications strategy that keeps everyone on the same page.
- **Don't bury the lead.** Keep the story of an ambition, a noble ambition, fresh and alive for external stakeholders.

## Embrace Reflective Practice

Most people are familiar with the famous Lucille Ball sketch of Lucy and Ethel in the wrapping department at a candy factory. As the belt speeds up, they resort to eating the candy, then stuffing candy into their hats and blouses. No matter what they do, they can't keep up. It must feel that way at many community colleges, especially in the last few years. As enrollments grew and budgets were cut the mantra of "doing more with less" became a demoralizing part of the campus lexicon. At the same time, the research in decision theory is quite clear. We are able, as individuals, to instinctively generate task lists in our brains. We have the capacity to know what is most important and what is least important. We also know that those things that are most important are usually also those that are the most complex and difficult.

In contrast, the simple tasks tend to be the least important. In a usual day, we often find ourselves returning phone calls, attending meetings and living, it would seem, on e-mail. And we go home exhausted by all the hard work we have performed. But what we have done, often unknowingly, is to attack the bottom of the list, those things that won't make much difference anyway, while letting the big, messy issues remain untouched and unsolved. The resulting "immediacy versus reflection" dialectic has been a part of philosophy since the Danish philosopher Kierkegaard. But it doesn't require us to delve through the approaches described by a 19th-century philosopher and others to understand this phenomenon. We all do it. We pass on the tough stuff while embracing what comes easy.

The findings embedded in the data described in earlier chapters are not particularly encouraging. In chapter 2 I noted that there was little acknowledgment of the scope of mission statements—what was included versus what was excluded. In chapter 3, I noted that many vision statements did not inspire any specialness (see Table 3.3) and that words such as *quality* and *excellence* were used too frequently (see Table 3.4). In chapter 4, I illustrated that values were too often merely a list of words (see Table 4.1). Furthermore, I pointed out that in most strategic plans there were few descriptions of the methodology used to develop mission, vision, and values, leading one to conclude that the processes might be less than rigorous.

This critique is surprising given that academe, almost by definition, should be thickly populated with reflective practitioners. One of the defining characteristics of professional practice, as originally defined by Donald Schon (1995) as "the capacity to reflect on action so as to engage in a process of continuous learning," which is one of the defining characteristics of professional practice. This practice-based learning is a function of professionals gaining insight from their own experiences, rather than from formal teaching or knowledge transfer. In education, reflective practice often refers narrowly to the process of professors studying their own teaching methods and determining what works best for the students. More generally, though, faculty, staff, and administrators should be studying their institutions, as professionals, to determine what is working, what is not, and how that relates to their stated ambitions.

Not only should we be reflecting, but also we should be investing significant time and energy in those reflective activities. This is another concept that should not be foreign to us. Perhaps the best example of this is the widely used "Seven Principles of Good Practice in Undergraduate Education" originally developed by Chickering and Gamson (1987). One of the seven principles states that "good practice emphasizes time on task":

Time plus energy equals learning. There is no substitute for time on task. Learning to use one's time well is critical for students and professionals alike. Students need help in learning effective time management. Allocating realistic amounts of time means effective learning for students and effective teaching for faculty. How an institution defines time expectations for students, faculty, administrators, and other professional staff can establish the basis for high performance for all. (p. 2)

Given the overwhelming challenge of reacting to daily problems, what can be done to ensure that we spend enough time on what matters most—our collective, indeed, our noble ambitions? The first and most important task that could be performed here is to be intentional about making a review of mission, vision, and values a discrete part of each new strategic plan. Typical plans have a 3- to 5-year cycle, moving from plan (developing the plan) to do (implementing the plan) to check (assessing the plan) to act (making changes to the plan). That final stage of deciding what to do next should entail deep dialogue about the efficacy of the stated mission, vision, and values to drive ambition, tension, and resolution. The result is a debriefing process (some people use the military term "after action review"), a structured review that analyzes *what* happened, *why* it happened, and *how* it can be done better, by the participants. Organizationally, it is also ideal to have a designated chief planning officer who ensures that reflective practice takes place within prescribed cycles (or have the appropriate duties assigned as part of someone's responsibilities). That same individual is tasked with organizing groups—e.g., a visioning team—who can commit the time needed to reflect on purpose, aspirations, and beliefs. Most importantly, reflection does not have to be the victim of immediacy. Wake Technical Community College, Fox Valley Technical College, and Houston Community College are examples of institutions that have demonstrated robust, well-documented institutional effectiveness functions in the face of demanding daily challenges.

# Make Words Matter

This promising practice, like the next one as well, flows directly from the conviction that if members of an institution really want it to stretch and grow, they need to devote more of themselves to exploring, clarifying, codifying, and then communicating their intentions to all the college's stakeholders. This particular practice focuses on one area that should be a significant part of those deep discussions—the language of ambition.

Again, this is something that academics should be good at. Think about survey courses in community colleges. These introductory courses cover an entire subject matter area, whereas advanced courses focus on narrower, more specialized topics. A large majority of the credit hours generated in community colleges come from several dozen survey courses. Those survey courses are designed to lay out basic concepts and present a lexicon for the discipline that can then be used as building blocks in exploring advanced concepts. We should be comfortable, then, with the idea of defining terms and being thoughtful about words and language because it is a large portion of the knowledge transfer we do in the core of theenterprise of learning and teaching. Why should we not be just as careful and precise when describing our institutional ambitions?

I believe there are at least three actions that could be taken. The first is what might be called "understanding the fundamentals." Even before getting into the deep dialogue that will eventually lead to describing your ambition, some time and effort should be devoted to enumerating the elements of that ambition and what they mean. I noted earlier in the book that some mission statements included institution wide goals that were not time- or task-specific as would be the case in a strategic plan. Others enumerated institutional student outcomes or a set of behaviors or competencies that graduates were expected to possess. Values were often described as guiding principles. It is not important, or even recommended, that individual institutions toe the line on a prescribed set of elements that define their ambition. What is important, however, is that those elements are the result of a conscious decision process and that the terms are defined.

For example, Naugatuck Valley Community College's 2010–2013

strategic plan, *Toward a Splendid College*, enumerates 5 goals, 15 initiatives, and 10 outcomes. What is key, foundationally, is that they define their terms: "Goals—*What we aspire to*; Initiatives—*What we will do*; and Outcomes—*What will be different by 2013*." Sauk Valley Community College is another institution that focuses on fundamentals. In their *Strategic Directions* document they also take a moment to define their terms before moving on to describe their ambition:

- Mission—*Tells who we are as an institution and what we do*
- Vision—*Tells where we want to go as an institution*
- Shared Ethical Values—*Tells how we do what we do*
- Goals & Objectives—*Strategic activities that will move the College toward its vision; Tactical activities that will enable the College to achieve its goals*

The second action is "don't be lazy." There appears to be an overwhelming tendency to be less than ambitious when speaking about ambitions. Again, the best example of this is the word frequency analysis showing that the words *excellence* and *quality* dominate vision statements. Words can and should help differentiate your institution from the college down the road or across town. Employees and other stakeholders want to be a part of something special. Some institutions have used words like *relevance* and *urban oasis of learning* to pronounce their distinctiveness. Naugatuck Valley's notion of a "splendid" college creates interest and promotes individuality.

Finally, "say more with less." I have noted that many mission statements exceed 400 words; the Gettysburg Address comes in at 272 words. There are no ideal word counts for mission, vision, or values statements. In general, though, parsimony pays. It pays because the reader doesn't get lost in the language and comes away with a feeling that the institution lovingly labored over each of the words. Take Harford Community College, for example. With less than 10 words—"We aspire to make our great college even better"—it manages to describe an institutionwide imperative that good enough is simply never good enough.

# Make Process Matter, Too

A final recommendation that can be used in the development phase of a college's ambition also requires another significant investment: The best mission, vision, and value statements are ultimately only as good as the process that was used to develop them. As Senge (2006) has noted in great detail, a compelling vision must be coupled with its being shared. Shared visions, in turn, emerge from personal visions—"This is how they derive their energy and how they foster their commitment." The unfortunate reality is that too often a vision statement is a product of a senior-level retreat to a comfortable, off-campus location. Then, the task becomes to get people to buy into the vision. This is backwards. A successful vision, one that excites and inspires, is the product of a lot of conversation that both resonates with the existing culture and creates a healthy, hopeful tension.

Another way to look at this is through the Malcolm Baldrige National Quality Award (2013) lens. Seven criteria are used to evaluate institutions and help them drive performance improvement. The most significant single criterion is results conferring 450 points (out of 1,000 total) along five dimensions—student learning; customer-focused; workforce-focused; leadership and governance; and budgetary, finance, and market. But the other 550 points are awarded under six other criteria that encompass process, that set of integrated approaches that when properly deployed will generate ever-improving results.

So, how should process be used to help advance a college's ambition? I believe there are four critical components to this promising practice: inclusion, transparency, feedback, and documentation. Inclusion is the obvious starting part. It is always important, especially in a college with all its nooks and crannies, to begin with broad, representative teams that provide the necessary perspective. Next, I especially like using technology to make the process transparent by using SharePoint or other collaboration software on an Intranet to describe the process and draft results as they are emerging. The next element, feedback, is used to expand the circle of engagement beyond the immediate teams by posting draft materials and asking for suggestions. The key is to ask. It is not likely that deep dialogue will erupt spontaneously. It more than likely will not. But asking is engagement just as a professor does in the middle of lecture—How are we doing? Make sense? Any questions? It helps to create an open, receptive environment and, every once in a while, a very cool idea does emerge, or a confusing one is clarified. Finally, there is documentation. It is important to codify what happened and also to continue to communicate, especially to external stakeholders, the process that was used to generate the results. Grossmont College, for example, has a college planning website that begins by explaining what it is all about from a process perspective:

> Our goal at Grossmont is to develop a culture that values the input of people in identifying those things that we do well, examining those areas where we can benefit from improvement, and utilizing data to inform the decisions that we make. The planning effort within the college strives to integrate the long-term vision and goals with the annual implementation of strategies by each college department or unit to achieve those goals. The accomplishment of those goals is measured and evaluated through a comprehensive unit review process.

The entire integrated planning cycle is laid bare—how the plan is developed, how the plan is implemented, and how evaluation (college level and unit level) is conducted. *The Grossmont College Strategic Plan 2010–2016* is included and further describes the specific strategic planning process used, including how it did environment scanning—"External trend analysis was conducted by teams of scanners focusing on four areas likely to have the most impact on the college and its community." The process also included, "At the same time, the entire college community was invited to participate in a visioning activity whereby the college reflected on its current successes and set a vision for the college in 2016."

## Be on a Mission

The background on mission statements in organizations was explored in chapter 1, as well as specific information on mission in institutions of higher education. Moreover, it was noted in Table 2.1 that having a mission is not optional in American colleges and universities. It is mandatory. But having a mission statement so that it can be checked off a list is very different from developing and implementing something that can help create a desired state that is embraced by an institution's stakeholders.

The promising practice I offer here is largely described in the work of Simon Sinek in *Start with Why: How Great Leaders Inspire Everyone to Take Action* (2011). Sinek uses his Golden Circle to explain. The outer ring is "what." It describes an organization's products or services. As such, whats are easy to identify. The next ring is "how." These are the factors that motivate or differentiate the products or services. They are more difficult to describe. The inner circle, the core, is "why." This is purpose, cause, or belief. Or as Sinek says, "WHY do you get out of bed in the every morning? And WHY should anyone care?" When most organizations or people think or act they do so from the outside in, from what to why. The primary reason is because the clearest thing, the easiest to comprehend, is the what. The fuzziest thing, the most difficult to define, is at the core—the why.

Community colleges are largely about the what. Check out the websites. They are jam packed with information about programs, catalogues, and schedules. Most colleges, even small ones, have hundreds of classes and dozens upon dozens of programs. And we offer the classes two or three times a year. That is a lot of product to push. Then there is the how. We have to get our students counseled and registered and a financial arrangement concluded. Moreover, some institutions have a statement on educational philosophy while others have goal statements that say things such as the following:

- ABC College faculty and staff are dedicated to helping students be successful. They emphasize excellence in teaching and providing a variety of support services that are designed to meet students where they are and help them reach their personal and professional goals. Beyond the classroom, the college provides for students a variety of co-curricular activities that serve to create a rich campus life experience.
- DEF College advances the economic development of the region through programs, services, and partnerships that address continuing and emerging employer needs in a diverse set of industries,

including one of the largest concentrations of entertainment studios in the world.

- GHI College hosts numerous cultural and athletic events throughout the year and serves as home to the XYZ Historical Museum.

That is quite a bit of what and how. But what about why? Sinek argues that why is the primary and most powerful motivator of human behavior but then explains that most organizations don't start there. They start with and stick with what and how. When you reverse the order, an entirely different dynamic is in play. Sinek uses the example of Apple. A marketing message from Apple, if it were to sound like everyone else, might sound like the following:

"We make great computers. They're beautifully designed, simple to use and user-friendly." Wanna buy one? (p. 40)

This approach focuses on products and features much like a community college pitching programs and a schedule that has evening and online classes. But what happens when the hard work and deep digging of why is the starting point? How did that allow Apple to develop such brand loyalty and universal respect for its operations? This time, the example starts with why:

In everything we do, we believe in challenging the status quo. We believe in thinking differently. The way we challenge the status quo is by making our products beautifully designed, simple to use and user-friendly. And we happen to make great computers.
Wanna buy one? (p 41)

A mission statement should, fundamentally, be about why—"Why do we exist?" Yes, it is the one element of an ambition that is universally required. But it is also the one element that gets to the very soul of the operation of your community college. Ask why. Keep asking it, five times, like peeling an onion, until you get at a basic understanding of why you do what you do. At that point, you should be able to answer another really key question: Do you just have a mission statement, or are you on a mission? You want to be on a mission. Harper College, has plenty of programs and classes to offer. It has processes to support them, too. But with its self-described world's most succinct mission statement, you might also safely conclude that it is on a mission . . . "Finish."

## Take the Road Less Traveled

Ideally, if you were to go on a college campus and ask a broad range of people the question "What makes this institution special?", you would hear similarities among the responses. The language would be the same, the sentiments would merge together and ring true, and the conclusion that you reached would be that, indeed, there is something special going on here. Having conducted this simple exercise on college campuses, I can tell you that what usually results is something quite different. The majority of the time the answers involve the idea that the college in question has really great instructors—"the teachers here are just wonderful." Now that may be the case at any single institution but as we know from A Prairie Home Companion's fictional town Lake Wobegon "where all the women are strong, all the men are good looking, and all the children are above average," it is statistically impossible that all professors at all colleges are "above average." Of course, what is happening is a distinctiveness deficit. Without a compelling vision that is widely shared, the fallback view is to state the obvious—not the road less-traveled as Robert Frost proffered but, instead, the road well traveled.

More than 20 years ago, Barbara Townsend took a stab at encouraging community colleges to step out of the shadows in her monograph, A Search for Institutional Distinctiveness (1989). As she observed then, "The benefits to a community college of undergoing a search for institutional distinctiveness include increased morale of institutional members and an improved image within the local community." This call to action has not been particularly successful. Research conducted by Abelman and Dalessandro (2008) led them to conclude that the institutional visions of community colleges are not very compelling—they lack "language intended to generate enthusiasm among stakeholders and stimulate them." The results contained in this research reinforce these conclusions. First, as noted earlier, the data reveal that terms such as *quality* and *excellence* dominate the phrasing in mission, vision, and values statements. This is a classic tautology—a needless repetition of ideas or words. For example, saying that you have high-quality faculty members (all above average), does not lead to the tortured conclusion that the institution must be excellent. Saying so does not make it so. In addition, it has been shown that too many vision statements appear to be virtually interchangeable (see Table 3.3).

Perhaps one of the reasons for the distinctiveness deficit is our inherently egalitarian nature. We are not great at "tooting our own horns" or making conscious decisions about how we can distinguish ourselves from our sister institutions of higher learning. Indeed, one of the many challenges facing community colleges in this era is mission drift. There are lots of things that we could be doing, but that does not mean that we should be doing them. It is simply tough for us to "just say no." Still, the promising practice here is to decide intentionally to opt for that road less traveled. That initially requires an institution—like Chief Dull Knife College, Los Angeles City College, and Clark State College—to give itself permission to be unique. That takes courage. Why? Because often the first reaction to a distinctive vision is that it doesn't sound like all the others. There is, after all, safety in numbers. Next, it requires an investment of time and energy because distinctiveness, as Townsend noted, is the result of a search or deep dialogue.

But it can be done. One of my favorite illustrations is one that I stumbled upon years ago. How could anyone develop a vision for a 125-year-old shipbuilding company that would inspire and resonate with its employees and their customers? Newport News Shipbuilding found the answer in the words and sentiments of its founder, Collis Potter Huntington—"We Shall Build Good Ships Here; At A Profit If We Can, At A Loss If We Must, But Always Good Ships." Years later, in speeches and workshops, I use Newport News Shipbuilding as an example of a compelling shared vision. I figure that if a shipbuilder can find a distinctive way to speak to excellence and quality, a community college should be able to do so as well.

## Do What You Say

As noted in the Introduction, individuals sincerely believe that values are important in an organizational setting. But it has also been shown that community colleges do not appear to spend much effort developing and communicating their values. The first recommendation, embrace reflective practice, spoke directly to enhancing the kind of dialogue needed to develop institution-specific values—that is, the belief system for an organization should reflect deeply-held principles that are part of the culture. Several other promising practices offered later in this chapter speak to communication approaches that can be used to advance this aspect of our noble ambitions. But there is one small problem. No matter how much effort is devoted to arriving at a common understanding of "what is good or desirable and what is not" and then having important conversations about those beliefs, what really matters is living those ideals.

The title of this promising practice is based on a classic book, *What We Say/What We Do*, by Irwin Deutscher (1973). The author, a sociologist, reviewed and analyzed dozens of experiments in which people were asked about something such as their views about drinking or racial attitudes. Then the experimenters watched their behaviors. The evidence was disturbing: People often did not do what they said and sometimes did just the opposite, leading Deutscher to conclude, "If we could not count on what people told us, then we had to be much more attentive to what they were doing." What happens in an organizational setting when what we say doesn't match what we do? What happens when the values we espouse as an institution aren't reflected in individuals' actions?

First, do not think for a moment that people aren't watching and listening. Throughout the day, in meetings and in memos, at events and in the hallways, the leaders of a college are showing what they value. How they speak, who they greet, and how they invest their most scarce resource—their time—reflects who they are and what they believe in. Secretaries, groundskeepers, registration clerks, instructors, and others pick up on the cues—intended and unintended, big and small. They do not miss much . . . and then they talk.

A quick example may help. In 2008, the University of Pittsburgh Medical Center (UPMC) rolled out a Dignity & Respect Initiative to its employees in an effort to promote inclusion through behavioral and organizational change. Employees were tasked with taking a pledge to demonstrate their commitment to treating others the way they want to be treated and providing their opinion on behaviors that represent dignity and respect in the workplace. Based on their feedback, "30 Tips of Dignity & Respect" were created. Awareness of UPMC's efforts spread beyond Pittsburgh, and a national "Dignity & Respect Campaign" was born. The development and growth of the initiative appears to have been organic, with the data for the resulting 30 Tips coming from the employees themselves. They arrived at a common understanding of what is good or desirable and what is not.

But what happens when the leadership of a community college in Texas or California grabs this idea and informs the faculty, staff, and administrators that they will be asked to take that same pledge? Remember, this is not their initiative. It comes prepackaged with someone else's language, tips, and pledge materials. I can tell you the first set of questions are "Do we have a problem with dignity and respect" and "Where did this come from?" But the real challenge is the what we say/what we do one. The past, present, and future behaviors of the leaders who imposed the pledge will be scrutinized. And hypocrisy is a killer. The word frequency analysis shown in Table 4.2 is very clear. Behind *student* and *community,* the words most frequently used by community colleges in their values statements center around the concept of trust. Values and trust are inseparable. What you say and what you do need to be inseparable as well.

## Keep Folding Things In

Our core elements represent a desired state . . . an ambition. When they are well developed and embraced by the members of the institution, the result is a tension between that ambition and the actual state. Without that tension and the actions that result—the resolution—the status quo prevails. Good enough is simply good enough.

The most immediate facet of resolution is making mission, vision, and values the key drivers associated with the strategic plan. Next, the plan needs to enumerate concrete action steps and assign units of primary responsibility to those actions to ensure that the tasks are completed in the appropriate timeframe. An even broader context, as we have noted, is described as institutional effectiveness in which assessments are completed (after action reviews) and changes made in a whole-systems, continuous improvement fashion. Understandably, this is not necessarily easy to do, especially in organizational structures like higher education that tend to focus on individual parts rather than the whole.

There are numerous useful metaphors to describe what needs to happen. Senge (2006) uses a large arrow and a set of smaller ones to illustrate the concept of alignment. The large arrow represents the purpose, the vision, of the organization. Within that large arrow, smaller arrows denote the interests and actions of individuals within the organization. In a first graphic, an illustration of an unaligned institution, the individual arrows are shooting off in all different directions. Some are even punching through the back of the big arrow headed in the opposite direction. "The fundamental characteristic of the relatively unaligned team is wasted energy," notes Senge. By contrast, when a team becomes more aligned, a commonality of interests and direction emerges. There is less wasted energy. Indeed, as is readily apparent from a second graphic, where the smaller arrows all align with the larger arrow, there is collective synergy as those individual interests begin to complement and reinforce one another.

For a community college, what this suggests is that the mission, vision, and values should be the beginning, not the end, of the conversation. Every day, hundreds of decisions are made by hundreds of individuals on everything from which courses and programs to offer to how financial aid disbursements are made. Those decisions require investments of time, energy, and money. As such, the ambition can and should act as a guide for decision makers. Indeed, it is not far-fetched to suggest that for every decision that is made, there should be a mental checklist used:

- Does the decision support the purpose that we have decided upon?
- Does the decision help us to create our intended future?
- Does the decision reflect how we have agreed to treat each other?

A second metaphor that I am fond of is the idea of "folding it in." Anyone who has spent any time in the kitchen is familiar with the technique. Two or more ingredients are brought together and, usually using a rubber spatula or wooden spoon, they are blended together using a light, gentle folding motion. The exercise is not as aggressive as mixing. To me, the mission, vision, and values of an institution are the core ingredients. Everything else—all the programs, policies, or personnel decisions, for example— needs to be made in the context of whether or not they can be "folded in." After all, the institution ultimately operates as a whole, so the question should always come back to whether or not the new ingredient is compatible with the other key ingredients. A glimpse of this type of "connected" thinking can be seen in Cascadia Community College's identity statement (see chapter 2) in which the concepts of vision ("we strive for a place where . . ."), mission ("we do this by . . ."), values ("we stand for . . ."), and learning outcomes ("we teach students how to . . .") are presented in an interlocking fashion.

Regardless of whether you use the image of arrows being aligned, or ingredients being folding into a recipe, this promising practice is focused on becoming intentional about the use of purpose, aspirations, and beliefs in developing strategic plans and making day-to-day decisions about the operations of your community college.

## Never Stop Communicating

One simple organizational development tool I have used in my consulting work is called a plus-delta. The approach is to place a large "T" on a flip chart with a plus sign over the left side and a change symbol over the right. Starting on the left side, individuals are asked to share what they think is good about the activity, unit, or organization. Much of this analysis taps into the Appreciative Inquiry approach (Cockrell, McArthur-Blair, & Schiller, 2012) by trying to identify what is working well and how an institution can do more of it. The right side focuses on what they would change in order to improve the same activity, unit, or organization. This analysis—seeking "opportunities for innovation and continuous improvement"—aligns with the language and approach used in the Malcolm Baldrige National Quality Award education criteria discussed throughout this book.

What is interesting is that in all types of institutions, facing all types of challenges, the dominant "change" item I have discovered involves communication—"No one tells me anything about what is going on around here." Too often this sentiment is couched in conspiratorial terms: The administration is purposefully trying to keep us in the dark. These perceptions are not benign, either, because this line of thinking is used to undermine difficult decisions that have been made by implying autocratic motives. The result is that decisions are never finalized. Even small decisions can end up lingering or festering for months and years.

Much of this "no one ever tells me anything" mantra can be attributed to the pigeonholing and loosely-coupled aspects of higher education discussed in the Introduction. We have departments and disciplines and sub-disciplines in which there is little incentive for investing in understanding and appreciating the "sum of the parts." And, in some ways, community colleges face an even greater challenge because, for us, the parts are always on the move. Our students, obviously, don't live in dorms, and most don't take a full load of classes—they come and go. Our faculty and staff mimic this kinetic behavior. Because of our low-cost structure and seasonal registration patterns, we hire large numbers of part-time registration assistants and advisors. Roughly half of all community college classes are taught by adjunct faculty who have minimal motivation to do anything but come, teach their classes, and go. And finally, full-time faculty members do not have scholarly research expectations that, at the university level, create an environment in which professors need to collaborate on a daily basis.

Given such a swirl, how can community colleges work to ensure that large numbers of faculty and staff be a part of developing, understanding, and advancing the purpose of institution and its distinctive aspirations and internalize a set of commonly-held values that create a powerful and empowering culture? The answer is that people need to be on the same page, and that does not just happen by itself. Both the page and the process for getting them on it need to be consciously designed.

One place to begin in your community college is to ensure that someone in the institution has "internal communications" in his or her job responsibilities. Like so many things, if it isn't someone's responsibility to design, monitor, and improve internal communications, it will usually falls through the cracks. The institution needs a coach to give people the communication tools and then to help them practice using those tools until they become part of the environment or "how we do things around here."

The next step is to create and implement an internal communications strategy. Houston Community College (HCC) has a four-part approach. The first part is "cascading what you know." It states that every staff meeting—up and down the organizational ladder—should begin with time devoted to "things you need to know." It should be obvious that if you start this practice at the senior executive level, then consistent messaging begins to cascade down the organizational chart. Mission, vision, and values, as well as how they are connected to strategic decision-making should then become part of that information flow.

The second part is "round-and-round we go." HCC has chartered 28 communities of interest or practice (Wenger, McDermott, & Snyder, 2003). While cascading helps to ensure top-down information flow, this initiative helps break down the barriers of our pigeonholed organizational structure. For example, if HCC states in its vision that it is focused on "relevance" and science, technology, engineering and math (STEM) programs are critical in a city like Houston, then having a STEM Council with dozens of faculty members and its own SharePoint site is a powerful way to advance horizontal information flow.

The next part is "shine your light, brightly." The power of storytelling was discussed in chapter 3 as a way to improve the stickiness of ideas. HCC works hard to encourage people and programs to tell stories that relate to the institution's purpose, aspirations, and beliefs. A communications person works with the area to shape the story and then the website, the Intranet, and the daily HCC News e-mail blast is used to spread the story. The final part is "Management by Walking Around." The trick is to shrink the size of organization by creating opportunities for intimacy—both sharing and listening. As has been noted, one of the most often identified value (see Table 4.2) was trust. You can't build trust while sitting in your office tucked behind your desk.

## Don't Bury the Lead

All journalists are familiar with the concept. You only have a small amount of time to capture the attention of continually distracted readers. So, you want to take the essential points or facts of the story and present them at the very beginning. Then, once you've hooked them, you have time to present the secondary materials in a deliberate way. But if you decide to lead with ideas of less-than-primary importance to the reader, you may never get the chance to tell the story that needs to be told. Higher education behaves as if its stakeholders were subscribers to academic journals—willing to plow through pages of literature review and methodology before getting to the kernel of the idea. We bury the lead of our noble ambitions.

It is clearly evident by now that we no longer have the luxury of sitting behind our proverbial ivy-covered walls and thinking great thoughts. Numerous surveys show that a majority of Americans say that higher education is unaffordable for most people and fails to give students good value. Headlines such as "Is College Worth It?," "Doing More With Less," and "Academically Adrift" are a staple for newspapers and book publishers. Legislators continue to want to put the words "colleges and universities" and "being held accountable" in the same sentence. Sensitivity to these externally focused topics should be paramount in the minds of everyone associated with community colleges because, after all, we are supposed to be more intimately connected, more responsive to our community, than our sister 4-year institutions. It should also be evident that being able to enumerate, clearly and concisely, the answers to our ambition questions should be a key part of that conversation. But there is little indication in this research that individual community colleges devote much time to the mission–vision–values dialogue, and there is less evidence to suggest that even if the requisite "time on task" was invested that it has led to an ambition-driven narrative that informs and animates external stakeholders.

There needs to be intentionality around the narrative of our purpose and our aspirations in particular. The first step to coherent storytelling is to do what was referred to in chapter 3 as forced prioritization. The initial part of this has to come from the leadership—a commitment to building the brand of the institution. This requires vigilance and constant reinforcement. Immediacy cannot be allowed to drown out what matters most.

Let's begin with websites, the primary portal to information about your college. If you have to use the search function to find the mission of the institution, you are burying the lead. If you have to follow a series of pull-down menus to uncover the hopes and aspirations of the college, you are burying the lead. If you have developed a set of institutional outcomes for your students and they appear only in board minutes or a college catalogue, you are also burying the lead.

That does not mean that mission, goals, outcomes, or vision need to be a banner headline on your homepage. But take a hard look at most community college websites as was done in chapter 1. Everything seems to take priority over what seemingly matters most. Bus passes, vacation announcements, twitter feeds, and basketball results all get their small patch of real estate. Perhaps the best example of how to put first things first in an electronic medium is Steve Krug's five-star book, *Don't Make Me Think: A Common Sense Approach to Web Usability* (Krug, 2006). Whether you are a graphic designer or a college president, individuals in community colleges need to get serious about forced prioritization and decluttering the message of the institution.

In addition to being intentional, a second aspect of this final promising practice is reinforcement. In politics it's referred to as "talking points." It is still not enough to develop ambition-related elements and place them in print or e-media. The key concepts and language of mission and vision must be constantly repeated in conversations and presentations. Whether it is making a speech at the Rotary Club or handing out business cards with the vision statement on the back at a conference, the essential idea is to keep a sharp focus on the core elements of the college and how you choose to describe its ambitions. After all, the work that community colleges are doing is noble. We change people's lives. We create different futures for entire communities. We have an important role to play in the economic, cultural, and social well-being of the country. That story needs to be front and center. Don't bury the lead.

## Conclusion

After an exhaustive listening tour, the 21st-Century Commission on the Future of Community Colleges issued a report with seven, powerful recommendations that involved redesigning students' educational experience, reinventing institutional roles, and resetting the system. The final paragraph of this authoritative document *Reclaiming the American Dream* is as follows:

Now community colleges are asked to take part in a great rebirth of America. The future of the nation is at risk, in part because of inadequate investment in our human capital. The development of human potential is what community colleges are all about. This is an issue that community college leaders and their partners must take up and make their own. For it is in grappling with the complexity of global issues that Americans can learn again the simplicity of human aspiration. It is in wrestling with uncertainty about the economic future of the nation that educators can reimagine the role of community colleges in reclaiming the American Dream. And it is in nurturing the struggling dream of America that community colleges contribute mightily to the futures of their students, their communities, and the nation. (AACC, 2012, p. 31)

This soaring rhetoric is directed at policymakers and the broad sweep of community colleges. The only question that remains is whether such noble ambitions can be translated into specific and purposeful actions on the campuses of more than 1,000 institutions. I believe the research, analyses, and promising practices contained in these pages will be of great use in that endeavor.

# REFERENCES

Abelman, R., & Dalessandro, A. (2008, April). The institutional vision of community colleges: Assessing style as well as substance. *Community College Review, 35*(4), 303–335.

Academic Quality Improvement Program. (2007). *Introduction to AQIP.* Chicago, IL: Higher Learning Commission.

Alfred, R., Shults, C., & Seybert, J. (2007). *Core indicators of effectiveness for community colleges.* Washington, DC: Community College Press.

American Association of Community Colleges. (2012, April). *Reclaiming the American Dream: Community colleges and the nation's future.* Washington, DC: Author.

Bennis, W. G. (2003). *On becoming a leader.* Cambridge, MA: Perseus Books.

Bryson, J. M. (1995). *Creating and implementing your strategic plan.* San Francisco, CA: Jossey-Bass.

Bryson, J. M., & Alston, F. K. (2011). *Creating and implementing your strategic plan.* San Francisco, CA: Jossey-Bass.

Calder, W. B. (2006, Fall). Education leadership with a vision. *The Community College Enterprise.*

Cameron, K. S., & Quinn, R. E. (2011). *Diagnosing and changing organizational culture.* San Francisco, CA: Jossey-Bass.

Carlson, S. (2010, February 2). Distinct visions and strong leaders can sustain troubled colleges, speaker says. *The Chronicle of Higher Education.*

Chickering, A. W., & Gamson, Z. F. (1987). Seven principles for good practice in undergraduate education. *American Association of Higher Education Bulletin, 39*(7), 3–7.

Clark, B. (1984). *The higher education system: Academic organization in cross-national perspective.* Berkeley, CA: University of California Press.

Cockrell, J., McArthur-Blair, J., & Schiller, M. (2012). *Appreciative inquiry in higher education: A transformative force.* San Francisco, CA: Jossey-Bass.

Cohen, A. M., & Brawer, F. B. (2008). *The American community college* (5th ed.). San Francisco, CA: Jossey-Bass.

Commission on the Future of Community College. (1988). *Building communities: A vision for a new century.* Washington, DC: American Association for Junior and Community Colleges.

Complete College America. (2011, September). *Time is the enemy.* Washington, DC: Author.

Complete College America. (2012). *Remediation: Higher education's bridge to nowhere.* Washington, DC: Author.

Covey, S. M. (2004). *The 7 habits of highly effective people.* New York, NY: Simon & Schuster.

Deutscher, I. (1973). *What we say/what we do: Sentiments & acts.* Glenview, IL: Scott, Foresman.

Downey, J. A., Pusser, B., & Turner, J. K. (2006). Competing missions: Balancing entrepreneurialism with community responsiveness in community college continuing education divisions. *New Directions for Community Colleges, 136.*

Fritz, R. (1989). *The path of least resistance: Learning to become the creative force in your own life.* New York, NY: Fawcett Columbine.

Fritz, R. (1999). *The path of least resistance for managers: Designing organizations to succeed.* San Francisco, CA: Berrett-Koehler.

Ginsberg, B. (2011). *The fall of the faculty: The rise of the all-administrative university and why it matters.* New York, NY: Oxford University Press.

Hamel, G., & Prahalad, C. K. (2005, July). Strategic intent. *Harvard Business Review.*

Head, R. B. (2011, April). The evolution of institutional effectiveness in the community college in institutional effectiveness. *New Directions for Community Colleges.*

Heath, C., & Heath, D. (2007). *Made to stick: Why some ideas survive and others die.* New York: Random House.

Jacobs, J., & Dougherty, K. J. (2006). The uncertain future of the community college workforce development mission. *New Directions for Community Colleges, 136.*

Keller, G. (1983). *Academy Strategy: The management revolution in American higher education.* Baltimore, MD: The Johns Hopkins University Press.

Kraemer, H. M. J. (2011). *From values to action.* San Francisco, CA: Jossey-Bass.

Krug, S. (2006). *Don't make me think: A common sense approach to Web usability* (2nd ed.). Berkeley, CA: New Riders.

Kuh, G. D., & Whitt, E. J. (1988). *The invisible tapestry: Culture in American colleges and universities.* Washington, DC: ASHE-ERIC Higher Education Series.

McKeown, G. (2012, October 4). If I read one more platitude-filled mission statement, I'll scream. *HBR Blog Network.*

Mellow, G. O., & Heelan C. (2008). *Minding the dream: The process and practice of the American community college.* Washington, DC: American Council on Education.

Miller, M. (2010, September/October). The new leader [Editorial]. *Change.*

Mintzberg, H. (1983). *Structure in fives: Designing effective organizations.* Englewood Cliffs, NJ: Prentice Hall.

Mintzberg, H. (1994). *The rise and fall of strategic planning.* New York, NY: The Free Press.

Mourkogiannis, N. (2006). *Purpose: The starting point of great companies.* New York, NY: Palgrave McMillan.

Mullin, C. M. (2010, June). *Rebalancing the mission: The community college completion challenge* (AACC Policy Brief 2010-02PBL). Washington, DC: American Association of Community Colleges.

Nanus, B. (1992). *Visionary leadership.* San Francisco, CA: Jossey-Bass.

National Center for Education Statistics. (2011). *Integrated postsecondary education data system (IPEDS) institutional characteristics survey* [Data file]. Washington, DC: U.S. Department of Education.

National Institute for Standards and Technology. (2013). *2013–2014 education criteria for performance excellence.* Gaithersburg, MD: Author.

Porter, M. E. (1980). *Competitive strategy.* New York, NY: The Free Press.

Ready, D. A., & Truelove, E. (2011, December). The power of collective ambition. *Harvard Business Review.*

Sanaghan, P. (2009). *Collaborating strategic planning in higher education.* Washington, DC: National Association of Colleges and University Business Officers.

Schein, E. H. (1985). *Organizational culture and leadership.* San Francisco, CA: Jossey-Bass.

Schon, D. (1995). *The reflective practitioner, how professionals think in action.* New York, NY: Basic Books.

Senge, P. M. (2006). *The fifth discipline: The art and practice of the learning organization* (2nd ed.). New York, NY: Doubleday).

Senge, P. M., Roberts, C., Ross, R. B., Smith, B. J., & Kleiner, A. (1994). *The fifth discipline fieldbook.* New York, NY: Doubleday.

Seymour, D. (1995). *Once upon a campus: Lessons for improving quality and productivity in higher education.* Washington, DC: American Council on Education.

Seymour, D. (2002). Link planning, improvement, and IR: Los Angeles City College. *New Directions for Institutional Research: Successful Strategic Planning.*

Seymour, D. (2011, September/October). Tough times: Strategic planning as a war canoe. *About Campus.*

Seymour, D., Kelley, M., & Jasinski, J. (2002). Link planning, improvement, and IR. *New Directions for Institutional Research: Successful Strategic Planning.*

Sinek, S. (2011). *Start with why: How great leaders inspire everyone to take action.* New York, NY: Portfolio/Penguin.

Skinner, R. A. (2010, September/October). Turnover: Selecting the next generation's presidents. *Change.*

Southern Association for Colleges and Schools. (2012). *The principles of accreditation: Foundations for quality enhancement.* Decatur, GA: Author.

Townsend, B. K. (1989). A Search for institutional distinctiveness. *New Directions for Community Colleges.*

Townsend, B. K., & Dougherty, K. J. (2006). Community college missions in the 21st century. *New Directions for Community Colleges, 136.*

Tromp, S. A., & Ruben, B. D. (2010). *Strategic Planning in Higher Education: A Guide for Leaders,* Washington, D.C.: National Association of Colleges and University Business Officers.

Weick, K. (1976). Educational organizations as loosely coupled systems. *Administrative Science Quarterly, 1–19.*

Wenger, E., McDermott, R., & Snyder, W. M. (2003). *Cultivating communities of practice: A guide to managing practice.* Cambridge, UK: Cambridge University Press.

# ABOUT THE AUTHOR

Daniel Seymour is currently a visiting professor at California State University, Channel Islands. His administrative assignments have been as vice chancellor at Houston Community College, executive dean at Los Angeles City College, and assistant to the president at the University of Rhode Island, where he earned tenure as a business professor. He has a BA from Gettysburg College and an MBA and PhD from the University of Oregon. He is the author of a dozen books and monographs on business and education. He lives in Santa Barbara, California.

# INDEX